Sharing our Wisdom

A Collection of Presentations by People in the Autism Spectrum

Editors
Gail Gillingham and Sandra McClennen

The Autism National Committee

Second Printing, 2008 - Reformatted Edition

All marketing and publishing rights guaranteed to and reserved by the Autism National Committee
P.O. Box 429
Forest Knolls, CA 94933
Bookstore: 1-800-378-0386
Website: www.autcom.org

Published for the Autism National Committee by
Sandra and Douglas McClennen
619 North Sheldon Road
Plymouth, Michigan 48170

ISBN # 0-9687863-2-4

Printed and bound in the United States by
Kase Printing, Inc.
13 Hampshire Drive, Unit 12
Hudson, NH 03051

This book is dedicated
to all those on the autism spectrum
who continue to live without a voice.

May your efforts pave the way
for you to join our mighty chorus.

Table of Contents

Table of Contents

Prologue

The Autism National Committee is the only autism advocacy organization dedicated to "Social Justice for All Citizens with Autism" through a shared vision and a commitment to positive approaches. Our organization was founded in 1990 to protect and advance the human rights and civil rights of all persons on the autism spectrum. In the face of social policies of devaluation, which are expressed through the practices of segregation, medicalization, and aversive conditioning, we assert that all individuals are created equal and endowed with certain inalienable rights, and that among these are life, liberty, and the pursuit of happiness. In order to achieve these rights for those with autism, the Autism National Committee advances the research, understanding and practice of positive relationships and communication-based approaches to supporting children and adults with autism. One of the ways in which we do this is by listening to those who have autism through their oral presentations and written words.

The messages of those with autism are of hope, love and strength, but they are being drowned out by a society whose media choose to focus on the voices of those who believe it is a "devastating disorder that destroys people's lives."

The personal relationships that we have built with those on the autism spectrum tell us otherwise. Autism is not devastating. Having autism produces strong, resilient people who, against all odds, are standing up for themselves, demanding the right to be heard and to be understood. These are people who face each day with a sensory system that takes in stimulation at a much higher level than that experienced by typical people, a body that doesn't move where and how one wants it to and often moves in unwanted ways, and a variety of untreated medical problems that have been largely ignored by a medical community which attributes the problems to autism rather than taking them seriously. People with autism are not sick. . . not retarded. . . not crazy. . . not alien. They are just different.

1

This book is an attempt to share their wisdom with the world. Members of the Autism National Committee have had the opportunity to hear many presentations given by people with autism, and we feel humbled by what they are teaching us. As only a limited number of people have been able to attend these presentations, we have taken this opportunity to collect and share some of them with you, the reader, to give you a broader and more realistic picture of autism.

When we began this project, we realized that there were a large number of presentations available. We decided on a mix of presenters—those who speak with their voices, those who type independently and those who use facilitation to communicate—in order to share as complete a picture as possible. (We have not included presentations by those who are already published. How to access books written by people on the autism spectrum is explained on page 221 under Further Reading.) We have included each person on the autism spectrum who has been a member of the Board of Directors of the Autism National Committee because of their dedication to our work. As you read these presentations, remember that most were written to be spoken rather than read which results in greater informality than is typical in written work.

Autism affects each individual in a unique way. The presentations that you are about to read demonstrate this uniqueness. Each journey is different. Those who have blossomed were those who were fortunate enough to grow up in communities in which they were accepted and where accommodations were made for their differences. Others were not so lucky. Our society bears the cost of these mistakes along with each of these individuals. Can we learn for the future?

Coping with autism requires accommodations in our world. Because reading a book depends on the visual system, we have made accommodations to avoid visual overload. These include the size of the book (6" by 9"), which decreases the length of each line; the cover, both color choice and design; and the font, which is easier to read, as it has been explained to us, because of its rounded corners rather than sharp angles.

We have also chosen to celebrate the variety in people's lives rather than produce a book that fits a predetermined form. When we requested biographies of the authors, they fulfilled this request in different ways. As with autism itself, you will see the unique description of each individual author.

This book would not be possible without the willingness of our twenty-two authors to contribute their words to this joint effort. We thank each of them. It also would not be possible without the support of the families and friends of these authors, who have made certain that their voices will be heard. Thanks to you, too. Together we are making the world a better place.

Gail Gillingham and Sandra McClennen
Book Committee for
Autism National Committee

Dan Treacy
Presentable

Just a few seconds of peace
A moment to feel some calm,
Kind words
make things more tolerable.
You see my hideous actions.
I'm reduced to being a pet
Yet you are not appalled
I spit and hum and yell
Can't you see there's more to me?
I see you looking at me
I loathe myself as you do,
So, tell me what to do to become
Presentable to you.

Ruth Elaine Hane

On a Clear Day

Originally presented at the Autism Society of America
Wisconsin State Conference in 1996

I am commemorating a one-year anniversary. I was diagnosed
with High Functioning Autism last July. Today, I will tell you
about this commemoration. I will talk about my sensitivity
to light, sound, touch, and deciphering. Then, tell about
some of the ways that are helpful in reducing my discomfort.
Each person with autism is unique; symptoms and, of course,
treatments vary. What is beneficial for me, may not be for
someone else.

Several things you may notice....I have very little facial
expression when I speak...although I am aware of this, it is
difficult to relax my facial muscles when I am concentrating on
choosing the right word, and adjusting for florescent lighting.
I have stage fright when I speak before a group and a fear of

losing my place.

This is the reason that I read my speech rather than talk using prompt cards. My dyslexia causes the words to "move" around on the page, the florescent lighting creates a delay in hearing my own voice. Nervous tension prevents me from efficiently selecting one of several words that I visualize. To help me process the words, I am using a blue transparency for an overhead projector to overlay my pages.

Distractions in the room may cause me to lose my concentration. If you do need to leave the room during the hour, I probably will stop talking and follow you with my eyes for a moment or two. This is not to embarrass you in any way. Feel free to leave if you have to, I understand that many times at a conference like this, circumstances may require that you leave. I will try not to let it distract me, or to take it personally.

Microphones that squeal are a problem too. Since I do not understand how radio waves cause feedback, I tend to move cautiously when I am wearing a radio microphone. I do not like applause because of my sensitive hearing. The random, percussive noise is painful. I usually cover my ears to avoid the assault on my system. This is the reason that I am requesting that you not applaud this morning. If you wish to show appreciation after my talk please stand. I will gratefully acknowledge you by bowing in gassho...like this! Gassho is silent applause, I receive your good wishes and you receive mine. We are showing mutual respect for one another. Without you to listen, my story would not be heard, and without me to tell it... you would not hear it. Thanks.

Being autistic has many problems! As Kermit the frog says, "It isn't easy being green!"

Last December while I sat on my living room sofa, writing a proposal for this presentation, it started to snow, the wind lifting the delicate flakes upward swirling them about until the city landscape became obscured. When the storm subsided, three or four inches of new snow blanketed the walks and

8

street. Looking out of my window at the now...clear day, I thought of the title for this presentation: "On a Clear Day," just like the song Barbara Streisand and earlier, Robert Goulet made so popular. "On a Clear Day...you can see forever."

This is true, most of us can see... on a clear day. But, when I do see, I wonder why I couldn't have seen the solution or answer sooner. When often as not, all of the pieces were right in front of me the whole while. Dr. Claresa Pinkola Estes, author of "Women Who Run With the Wolves," is a senior Jungian psychoanalyst and an award-winning poet. She proposes on her audiotape, "The Creative Fire," that mistakes are not to be viewed as failures, but, rather an integral part of the creative process. She states, "Failures often lead the way to change...a window will open in a blank wall that couldn't be seen before."

As a dress designer, I know this is true; many times what seems to be a mistake in a design, a dismal failure, is nothing more than part of the design process. A brilliant concept, or a new idea will reveal itself as I tear out the seams and re-stitch it. Many times, eureka happens as a result of struggling with perplexing problems.

Autism is one of these perplexing problems about which we struggle. It is my wish that in recounting my experiences that windows of change will begin to open in a blank wall. I am here to offer hope, no matter how bleak the prospect seems today.

This session will give you a glimpse into my world; what it is like to be a person with High Functioning Autism. As it happened, I grew up with autism and dyslexia and nobody knew it. I never wanted to be different. I just was different... odd.... unusual.... perplexing.... daydreamer.... precocious and I didn't have a clue as to why I was. My life was a series of sentences without structure. The fabric pieces right in front of me could not be assembled, pieced, into whole cloth.

After the snow storm, I looked out of the window at the silent street, the snow mounded gently on the evergreen bushes, and suddenly remembered one of my favorite activities when

I was a small child...playing with glass paper weights.

I often visited Mr. Sorenson, a neighbor who was retired from farming potatoes all his life. I rang his doorbell twice just to hear his Westminster Cathedral chimes go through their melodic pattern. His wife working in the house called out, "No need to ring twice, we heard you the first time! Come on in." Mr. Sorenson enjoyed children and let me look at his collection of glass-dome paperweights, if I was careful.

I studied each glassy sphere with a tiny winter scene inside. When I inverted the transparent object, flakes of snow drifted to the top, then, when I righted it, the artificial snow settled onto the little village or miniature farm scene inside. When I was five or six years old I became fascinated with these paperweights, turning them over and over watching the snowfall, my eyes level with the table's edge lost viewing the fairyland inside. I could do this for hours and not become bored. I became obsessed with finding them. I played with the glass domes wherever I went...I wandered into my friend's houses, looked for them at the neighbors, and the corner nick knack store. However, much to my dismay, some people... wouldn't let me touch their collection of paperweights. When this happened I made a terrific fit, kicking and screaming for twenty or thirty minutes if I couldn't have my way. Looking at paperweights was one of my many fixations.

Fixation, or perseveration, is one of the symptoms of autism. I will tell you stories about myself that illustrate other typical symptoms as well. My hope is that you will relate to my stories, and that perhaps you can find some humor in them. Laughing and finding humor is healing, opening a window for change.

Now I want to talk about improving. I intend to grow and change until the day I stop breathing and die. One of the ways that I improve is by watching carefully, and then asking countless questions...such as...Why do you do that? What for? Who would want to do that? Really! How strange, well OK, but I can't imagine it! Then, I'll try it out for myself and decide.

Getting along socially is a problem. I could not read social cues easily. I learn by observing people, then practice what others do in various situations, even though it feels unnatural to me at the time. These are social skills that most people acquire easily as they live; ones that I consciously make an effort to learn. Now, with the help of many years of psychotherapy, and by reading books on behavior and helpful family and friends, I usually respond positively to criticism and try to change my behavior. One of the things I am trying to change is to use more transition words to introduce a new subject or add to a conversation. I tend to be too direct, which can come across as critical or impolite,

My social skills improve every day, including the complicated ways that rules change when a situation is slightly different, and, a subtle nuance causes the appropriate response to be different. An example of this is a simple question..."How are you?" and the many ways this question changes through inflection.

For instance, when you see a long lost friend...You may say with shared enthusiasm "How ARE you!" or if you live in my state, "How are you, anyway? Well, gosh, it's been just AGES since I saw you last!"

Conversely, if a person were depressed after being laid-off from their job, you would say it with sympathy "How are you? Implying...How can I help? Or, if someone is celebrating a "decade" birthday of 30, 40, or 50, and the person dreads getting older, with a combination of empathy and possibly good humor. How are you? With a quiet voice and "sincere" manner. (Very complex.)

If these skills do not develop naturally, it takes a concerted effort to learn them. Kari Dunn, Autism Specialist in the Roseville School District of Minneapolis, is skilled in developing effective social stories to help children surf the maze of social interaction.

When I have concerns about a social situation, I ask for advice from someone whom I believe I can trust and is knowledgeable. Then I practice, practice, practice; learning from my mistakes, and apologizing if I have offended someone.

Zig Ziglar, the famous motivational salesman who lectures around the world on the subject of "making mistakes," reframes mistakes, calling them, "learning opportunities!" Zig Ziglar states in his rousing speeches that statistically, it takes nine mistakes for each success. Nine no's for every yes! Remember this when you feel discouraged. Try nine times before you expect a success...and quite possibly, he said, then there will be eighteen disappointments before there are two successes or thirty-six and four. The whole idea is not to give up...to keep trying.

Now, some history..."It isn't easy being green."
I tried for many years to find out about myself. After a life-long search for some explanation about the reason I feel different, I called the director of the Autism Resource Network, Cherri Saltzman, who suggested that I make an appointment with someone she trusted, a licensed psychologist in Minneapolis. Cindy Dolby Nollette is a specialist in diagnosing and treating people with autism.

The psychologist asked countless questions about my development, sensitivities to light, noise, touch, my resistance to change, my delay in understanding words spoken to me. She has diagnosed hundreds with autism, and knows what to ask and how to observe differences.

When our session ended, I expected her to schedule another appointment; instead, she paused for a long time before clearing her throat. I looked out of her office window while I waited. Then she said, "I believe that you are High Functioning Autistic. I have never been more certain of a diagnosis."

She commented on the many ways that a diagnosis of autism describes my symptoms. She complimented me on my patience and willingness to answer her detailed questions. Then, she asked, "How have you learned to compensate so well?" I replied honestly, "I don't know."

As I pulled out into traffic onto France Avenue after our

session, an ambulance blasted its siren behind me. I negotiated across several lanes of the busy street to get out of the way. Then I felt the dreaded pain at the back of my head radiating throughout my body. As I re-entered traffic I knew that I needed to be extremely alert, driving with caution until the pain subsided.

Suddenly it occurred to me that this is one of the ways I have learned to compensate...to concentrate and drive with great care after my nervous system is stressed. Continuing on my drive home, the pain lessened, and I began to think of a way that I could discover more about myself.

I decided to write about my experiences. Writing gives me access to scattered pieces of information, which I assemble into a whole, creating a continuity of my memories. I am presently writing a book about growing up with autism.

I did not want to be labeled autistic! Like many of you who have heard the diagnosis, I had mixed feelings. I felt sad and angry that it took such an arduous search to find out about autism. At the same time, I felt hopeful to have a direction to go in my search to improve my lot in life.

In many ways I consider myself lucky...because people seem to like me. *I do not take credit for this.* Some children, I believe, have a naturally attractive manner, or *charisma.* Others aren't so lucky.

The lucky ones, like I was, were given a greater chance to thrive. Many people made a difference in my life...teaching me what I needed to know to live, helping me find out about the practical things that I needed to learn. They indulged me in my curiosity and cared enough to correct me repeatedly, when I was wrong or did dangerous things. They were my parents, a nurturing neighbor, an elementary school principal, a nurse, a Zen priest, and a college professor. Presently, I continue to be lucky with many others helping me. I am grateful that somewhere in my makeup I could stop long enough to listen to my mentors and to find the will to learn and change. I want to say more about this...will to change. Besides having an immature brain that operated in a disjunctured way, I lacked the desire to conform to rules and expectations. I lacked a volition or will to act. I believe that breakthroughs will come in autism if we can discover how volition occurs, of how a neurological process happens.

I know that many times when I experience a paradigm shift in my thinking...that I have acted on the very slightest urge to do so...really just a wisp...a butterfly as I call it... Can you understand? I discovered in therapy, that I do not have the desire to change unless of course I am seeking something pleasurable for me. Then I can preservere until I get my way.

In order to help children with autism, I think that we must observe and watch carefully to catch them in this inclination, at the split second that it happens and give patient, loving encouragement. To re-enforce the wisp...until a greater reward, is comprehended. One that includes delayed gratification such as following rules, reading and learning personal skills.

Now I'll tell you about myself today. Presently I am fifty-five years old, a designer, an artist, writer, consultant, floral arranger, wife and mother to four children in a blended family. I volunteer for several organizations. I like to garden and have a pond. I enjoy cooking and baking and collect cookbooks. We have cats and goldfish. I am an insatiable reader. My daughter jokingly suggested a magazine and books anonymous group for me. My daughter is correct; I do have too many magazines and books.

As I said, I have learned to act fairly normal, so that I fit in most of the time. I grew up in a family of six children, I am the second child - for those of you who like birth orders. My parents were both highly intelligent, although under achievers by many standards. They believed that their lives were directed by God and were devoutly religious. My father, a borderline personality, had two distinct faces...one gentle and quiet, the other full of rage. My mother had several nervous breakdowns, as they were called in the 1950's, rendering her useless until she got away from the stress of housework and raising children.

In many ways, I feel that my parents were poorly suited to adapt to me and my special needs. My mother's health was generally poor. She secretly hoped that her pregnancy with me would end in a miscarriage; several times during the spring and summer she was certain that it would. My mother contracted German measles during her third month of gestation and nearly died of the fever. She recovered, but was overwhelmed, trying to parent my older sister while working to support my father until he finished Court Reporter's School in Chicago. When he graduated they moved to South Dakota.

My life began in Winner, a small town in Southwestern South Dakota. It was a frontier area at the time, with rolling open prairies. The cowboys, ranchers and Indians were feuding over some of the land boundaries; there were bar brawls and fights nearly every night.

I was born the day after a bleak Christmas in 1940. I forever changed my parents' lives. My nerve center was underdeveloped, and messages were scrambled. Flailing and crying, I screamed for the first twenty-four hours. Nothing consoled me. The kind and experienced head nurse gave up trying to calm me and to help me nurse. My mother said she looked sad, and seemed relieved when it was time for my mother to take me home.

I could not suck or swallow and was intolerant to my mother's milk. A neighbor in Winner arrived at a solution... to prop me on an oven-warmed flannel blanket, use a bottle filled with diluted goat's milk, and a large rubber nipple. With this plan, the warmed milk could drip down my throat. I was nourished even though I couldn't nurse. She said that she had saved many farm animals this way and was quite certain it would work for me. My life today is proof that it did. I am glad that she was willing to offer help.

Mother said, "You were a very peculiar infant. Didn't like to be held by anyone. You would struggle to get away when anyone who tried to hold you." Batting my blue eyes constantly, my straight dark brown hair and vacant cherub look attracted attention. When I fell asleep and anyone commented on my looks, Mother said, "Although she looks like an angel, don't be fooled into thinking she is." Most of the time, I was restless. As early as 3 months, when anyone propped me on his or her lap, I would squirm to get away, crying the entire time, while slipping to the floor.

When I was five months old, my older sister, mother and father moved, taking me to Brookings, South Dakota, where they rented a house on 8th Avenue. Our new neighbor, Ida Van Monen, lived so close that we shared a driveway. She was the mother of two girls and a great homemaker. This is how I remember Ida, by her house. It had window boxes with red geraniums, and a spotless flowered gray linoleum floor, with bright, white lacy curtains in all of her windows. She followed a weekly routine of cleaning, cooking and sewing.

We settled into our little, woodsided house with its small front stoop. It was a warm spring and our bedroom windows were raised to let in the fresh air. My continual crying was a problem for our neighbors who also had their windows open.

One night, about 2 am, Ida crossed the gravel driveway between our houses wearing her silk kimono bathrobe, her hair in pin curls, knocking on our back door. She said, "Let me take the baby, no one can get any sleep, what with all of the racket!" My mother, relieved that someone offered to help, shoved me toward her. Ida lifted me onto her shoulder, and magically I snuggled against the silky fabric of her robe. She had a way with babies is what the neighbors said. Ida rocked me vigorously in her rocking chair. She observed what things seemed to calm me. She let me decide how much touch I wanted or could tolerate. Years later she took me by the hand to show me the path she had worn in the linoleum floor rocking me that summer.

My crying and flailing continued. I did not crawl or develop in other ways, but rather scooted along, crab-like, on my side. Neither did I learn to coo or baby talk. Then at nine months I stood up, climbed stairs, walked and ran... all in the same day. This is the story my mother liked to tell.

When I was nine months old, my grandfather died in Chicago.

This meant that my parents drove our family from Brookings to Chicago for the funeral, an eleven-hour drive without air conditioning... and I did not like to be held. I traveled the whole trip down on the floor of the car, crying and throwing up. When my parents arrived at the house in Chicago, I was dirty, with sweaty matted hair, a filthy dress and a soiled-wet cloth diaper. My parents were frazzled.

Several aunts and cousins in my father's large family tried unsuccessfully to hold me. I screamed at the violation of my personal space. I wanted to be left alone. I scooted on my side hiding underneath chairs and furniture. Mother later told me that if I needed to turn over, I flipped over crab-like. My right arm extended above my head, then flip.

Later in the day, after the funeral, my father's entire family was gathered at an uncle's farm and vineyard. Tempers were short in the heat of the summer day, relatives were shouting. They were arguing about the family estate, the shortage of funds and who would pay for the funeral. I continued to cry and would not let my cousins play with me, insisting instead to scoot on my side underneath the dining room table where the family was seated. As the afternoon progressed, the angle of the sun shifted to hit the chandelier creating a prism of rainbow colored light at the top of the stairway adjacent to the dining room. Mother said that I scooted toward the light, reaching upward trying to touch it. I lifted my body up the first step and then up each step until I was sitting in the light at the top. My parents found me basking in a rainbow of light. At first they didn't realize my accomplishment, thinking instead that one of my cousins had carried me up there. They brought me back down the steps and into the dining room. This is NOT what I wanted. I wanted to sit in the light. Up I climbed over and over.

Later, after the funeral lunch that day, some family photos were taken. Afterward, I was missing. It didn't take them long to find me standing in the grape vineyard clutching a wooden vine while I ate the sour grapes. My father was embarrassed because of my odd behavior, saying I couldn't walk before I crawled, that it just wasn't natural. When he discovered me in the vineyard, he reached out in anger, to scoop me up. I dreaded being held by him since he held me so tight that at times I quit breathing. I twisted away from his grasp, turned, and to the astonishment of my relatives ran on my tiptoes to get away. My grandmother rescued me, holding me gently against her silk dress. She told my father that she would care for me until it was time for us to return home.

So, as the story goes... I stood up, climbed stairs, walked and ran... all in the same day. Recently, I read in a book, "When Snow Turns to Rain," about another autistic child, Jordan, who started walking at nine months too.

My speech was delayed. I used low guttural noises to communicate, or body language to get my needs met. By the time I was three years old, I could make four sounds: *ma, da, na, cum.* Everything else I communicated by pointing, dragging someone by the hand, or by screaming in a low penetrating screech.

I had no concept of a ME as a person, but rather thought I was a piece of furniture, or a washing machine, a clock, a wagon or a wheelbarrow, or a cat. Swish-swish, whir, tick tock, squeak and meow. I mixed pronouns, repeating what I was told to do, saying, "You want to go outside" if I wanted to go outside, thinking you meant me, although I didn't have an understanding of a me or an I.

This is the story about an unusual kind of talking... One Sunday, when I was four years old, I had the use of four or five short words, or pointed to communicate. My older sister dragged me to her Sunday School class explaining, "This is RuthE, she doesn't talk." I was to stay in the class while my parents attended church services. This became the customary arrangement.

Often I wandered away from the classroom, exploring on my own in other parts of the church building. My teachers learned to expect this, were unable to keep me in the classroom and let me wander. On this particular Sunday I was drawn to the foyer of the church by loud angry voices; one of them I recognized as my father's. Darwinism and the new theory of evolution was the unusual topic of the day's sermon....splitting the congregation irrevocably between the Creationists and the Evolutionists that day. My father espoused the Creationist view. He and the minister were having a shouting match. I stood, unnoticed, next to my father, taking it all in. Suddenly, I puffed up my small chest and in a deep tenor voice repeated the last sentence of what the minister shouted "Darwin and evolution is RIGHT! We evolved from the apes!" I repeated this over and over all the way to the car. As an added annoyance, I repeated this for weeks! I didn't know what I said. I believe that I was drawn to the strong emotion behind the sound of the words.

I have later learned that this is called echolalia. I continued to make elementary noises to express my needs, but now I believe that I had found the use of my vocal cords so that I could create a wider range of sounds. Slowly I learned to have meaningful speech.

When my sensory system became overloaded, I would crash....go blank, much as a computer does. I called it my nothing world, with no time or space, I could hear, see and be touched and not react to anything. Sometimes I remembered, other times, I did not. The voices seemed distant... tunnel-like. At these times, no words formed in my mouth to respond, nor, did I feel any desire to form them.

Dancing in the Streetlight

My nothing world was filled with magic! Snowflakes were drifting in the streetlight, glinting wildly as they floated past, making fairy tale rainbows of sparkling diamonds. Crystal prisms formed kaleidoscopes of shimmering lights. Stretching my arms out widely, palms upward, I danced and twirled as I gathered my snowflake friends on my mittens, watching as they melted, each tiny facet disappearing into the knitted wool. Unaware of a "far away" sounding voice of the shopkeeper, Ruth West, who was my neighbor, I see a navy blue gabardine skirt and blouse standing nearby. Mrs. West is telling me,

"It's getting dark and you must start walking home. It's ten blocks and bitter cold out here."

On other frigid afternoons, she would see me pressing my nose against the glass display windows, my eyes squinted to fracture the colorful Christmas lights reflecting in the piles of snow on the ledge. She guided my body inside to warm a bit, before she nudged my shoulder, pushing me in the direction toward home. At some level I sensed her concern for me. When I stood inside the store, my black buckle boots dripped snow onto the carpet. My green wool coat, worn at the cuffs, the collar turned up against my cheeks contrasted with the fashionable clothing hung neatly row upon row. The comforting smell of wax and polish making me want to stay forever... transfixed. Somewhere in my cloudy thinking, I remembered Mrs. West's kindness, the smells and fabulous colors. Years later, when I learned to sew clothing for myself, I decided to become a fashion designer to discover how to design and create these wonderful clothes.

Many days passed when my head felt fuzzy and thinking escaped me. Somehow I patched together information about foods that I ate that helped me think more easily. Mostly my motivation rested in finding the Mason jar filled with lumpy brown sugar that my mother hid from me. I knew that when I found the sugar and ate some, my head would be clear and calm. I remembered that I felt this way after eating certain foods.

Chard

One of my favorite stories is about chard, a nutritious green, leafy vegetable, high in vitamin content. When I was just four years old, I did not have a concept of me as a person, and antonyms, words that had several meanings, words such as ball and bawl (a ball to throw and to cry) were confusing. The reason that I tell stories with lots of detail is because I think in pictures and I remember objects more then people; the description of things give me cues to recall the people.

Our nice neighbor lady, Lila, had white curly hair and loved to garden. She wore crisply ironed housedresses with floral patterns printed on them. She cultivated beautiful flowers and vegetables in the moist, rich black soil in her side yard. She planted several rows of red and green leafy chard each spring. Her grass was lush and thick. I heard Craig say that she paid a boy twenty-five cents to pull the weeds and mow her lawn every Saturday. I loved to roll down the sloping hill beneath her window, the smell of Spice Cookies baking, warm sun and cool dirt intoxicating to me. I added hill rolling to my daily routine. Over and over I rolled down her hill.

One day, Lila briskly crossed the gravel road in front of our house. I watched from the sandbox in our side yard. She walked with such determination that the pink cotton skirt of her dress swished back and forth. Lila climbed our wooden steps to knock on our front door. I could overhear her as she talked to my mother. I sneaked around to hide behind the trunk of our tall spruce tree so that I could see her, too. She seemed upset and was complaining to my mother that she thought a raccoon must be the one spoiling her garden. She said the little rascal was pulling out the chard by the fistfuls. She waited up several nights to see if she could catch him and then try to chase him away.

One afternoon, I went to her garden to see if I could find the raccoon, since I had never seen one. Sitting quietly on the green grass covering the knoll next to her garden I waited and watched. I could hear the clink of Lila's dishes as she washed and dried them, probably placing them neatly in the cupboard. I had seen her tidying up her kitchen once before while I drank the cherry Kool Aid she had poured for me. My mother had sent me to borrow a cup of white sugar. Sitting on her kitchen stool, I had watched as she pulled the sugar canister down off the upper shelf, to ladle out the amount my mother needed to bake rhubarb pie. Sugar was rationed during the war.

Perhaps if I sat very still the raccoon would come close enough for me to see the dark rings around its eyes or if I listened carefully, to hear the sound of the rings on its tail.

Looking out of her open, kitchen window, my neighbor exclaimed, "Well I never saw anything like this before." Bustling outside to her side yard to get a better look, she was drying her wet hands on her apron. She saw me sitting on her grass, eating fistfuls of crisp chard, the clumps of black dirt soiling my dress. I was eating the bitter-tasting greens, dirt and all, while I waited to see a raccoon. My neighbor exclaimed, "Good grief, Ruthie, is that you eating my chard? I thought it was the raccoons. Do you like chard? I never saw a child who wanted to eat chard before. You are an odd one. Well, dear, you can have all the chard that you want! Here, let me show you how to pinch the leaves so you don't pull out the rest of the plant."

At the time I didn't understand that I was the raccoon who was spoiling Lila's garden. The other neighbors told this story with great amusement that I couldn't comprehend. The next summer she planted an entire row of chard, just for me to eat. I did not like the bitter taste, but somehow I remembered that, I would feel better, would be more awake, and understand words spoken to me after I ate it. It wasn't until I wrote about this story, that I put the pieces together. Without a sense of a self I could not understand.

Other odd cravings I had were spinach, eaten directly from the can, cooked liver, baby carrots from the garden, asparagus, and green rhubarb stalks. I drank milk-of-magnesia straight from the blue bottle, until my mother discovered me doing it, and hid it from me. Undeterred, I went to several of the neighbor's houses to drink the milk-of-magnesia they had in their medicine cabinets.

I grew up in an age where doors were left unlocked, and screen windows left wide open. Keys were left in the car's ignition, windows down. Neighbors dropped in on one another, unannounced. Kids were welcome to knock, call their name and then walk in. "Yoo-hoo, it's RuthE! Is anybody home?" gained me entrance. Neighbors looked out for everyone's children. This is how I received most of the parenting that I needed. If I was missing, and I frequently was...my mother called around the neighborhood to see who had seen me last. I could be missing for several hours.

I loved apples and I ate oranges down to the bitter rind. I chewed on the nub ends of my teacher's chalk and ate white paste. I find this interesting, in light of some recent studies on trace elements and vitamins as contributing factors in neurological function. I probably needed added amounts of calcium, iron, magnesium, folic acid and other vitamins.

Recess

I was constantly in motion - rocking, skipping, running, swinging, twirling, dancing! Someone suggested to my parents that I might settle down if I could get an early start in Kindergarten. My December birthday was past the deadline date of Labor Day, nevertheless, I was enrolled after passing a test to see if was mature enough for school. I toured the room, saw the story telling, braided rug, blue cubby for my nap rug and showed little interest until I scored in sand and water. I did my best in what turned out to be a fixation...sand and water play. Apparently I was ready.

Walking the eight blocks by myself, many mornings I didn't make it all the way to school, being attracted by some diversion or other. If I did make it to school, often I would leave the schoolyard at recess, not understanding what going out for recess means. When my class went out to the playground, I would amble along, swing on the swings, walk on the top of the trapeze bar, climbed high into a tree, then dropping down from a branch landing deftly on my feet. One event lead to another...soon I was squatting, walking like a duck as I looked for perfectly round pebbles to add to my stone collection, that I carried in the front pocket of my dress. It didn't take long until I was two blocks from school, downtown, at my favorite dime store, where I liked to arrange the merchandise in the small wooden bins at the Woolworth's.

I especially liked to reorganize the kitchen gadgets. Among them were salt and pepper, shakers, chickens, green and brown frogs, pink or gray pigs and wooly looking sheep, all with little holes punched in their heads. I lined them up by color and height, using the partitions as stalls. I played with the nested measuring spoons, which made a lovely tinkling sound when I jiggled them. I think that my favorite gadgets, were the aluminum sprinkler tops with a cork bottom. (We did not have steam irons or permanent press or dryers then, so our mothers sprinkled the clothes before ironing them.) I loved to blow through the tiny holes of the sprinkler tops making a whistling noise, or to spin them on the wooden floor.

The clerks were not pleased with my "helpful" rearranging of their stock, since all of the prices were marked on the wooden partitions and not on the merchandise. This caused a lot of confusion at the checkout counter when their customers argued about prices. "But the bin said twenty-five cents, how can it be seventy-five?"

Each day, the clerks would march over to the black phone on the wall to call the principal and say, "Shee'ss here again!" A tall man in a blue uniform, the school truant officer, would come to find me to bring me back to my class. We stopped in the café for a five-cent cup of coffee for him. The next day I repeated this, ending up at Woolworth's, again! My wandering and odd behavior became a routine for everyone.

Following the rules for crossing streets by myself was a major problem. I could not judge the distance or speed of the cars and, not wanting to do it wrong and get a scolding, I waited until there were no cars in any direction to cross. This could take a long time! I would pivot my head back and forth vigorously, checking for any cars, but I couldn't trust my seeing and deciphering senses to be sure it was O.K. to cross. Usually some kind person would stop to help me. OR, I would cross in the middle of the block, thinking that no rules applied there!

School

Most days in kindergarten, I refused to leave the water table or the sand play. I could not sit still on the story rug and listen quietly while my teacher read a story. I understood the words better if I had an activity to do. I liked to play with the sticks of red clay, making elaborate figurines. I could cut with scissors, paste carefully and thread a small needle and sew. I saved toilet paper cores from the bathroom to add chimneys and smoke stacks, tunnels and windows to my sand castles. On the other hand, I did not understand up from down, left from right, now from later, before from after, over from under, stop from go.

When I was bad, broke a rule, or couldn't sit still, I was sent to the cloakroom to stand in the corner. On days when the weather was rainy or snowy, I hid in the fire escape at recess. I was promoted into first grade in the hope that I would mature to grade level over the summer break. I didn't, but was passed on to first grade anyway.

My second grade teacher was mean. She pulled at the back of my collar and commanded, "Sit up straight, pay attention, listen when I give directions, quit fidgeting, stop looking out of the window, don't day dream, read the words, don't look at the pictures. LOOK at the WORDS!" ...then whap across my face. Words made no sense to me. Little black, squiggly dots and lines swam across the page, at times, disappearing altogether if stared at too long. My face, mirroring the white page, revealed the blankness in my world. The classroom giggles; slaps and loud words no longer mattered to me, as I drifted off into my world. She passed me on to the next grade, glad to be rid of me I think.

During the third grade, a traumatic event occurred for me, because I thought that I could read but... actually, I couldn't. During the fall, the school board voted to change the entire curriculum, going from a phonics based system which used Dick and Jane books, to some experimental method of whole word recognition. This meant that when we returned from the Christmas holiday we would have all new books in math and reading. I did not like change and worried during the break about the new books we were to have. When I arrived at the classroom, the dreaded books were sitting on top of my desk, two brand new books, one for reading and one for arithmetic.

I plugged my nose to get rid of the new book stench.

My teacher called on me to read first. I looked puzzled. No one had read the story to me. I didn't know what the story was. I stared at her not knowing what she wanted me to do. After a long time, her voice prodding me to start. I improvised an interesting story, getting ideas from looking at the picture. Our class erupted into gales of laughter at my inventive story. The other kids often laughed at my peculiar ways.

The truth was that   I could not read a single word! My teacher scolded me for behaving like a "smarty pants" and sent me to the principal. Temporary amnesia they thought. Until this horrible day I had been one of the best "readers" in the third grade class. I could not read a single word, nor could I see letters to understand what the word "reading" meant. I had memorized every story, word for word, through the middle of the third grade.

My teacher tried unsuccessfully, to teach me how to read but eventually threw up her hands one day, as I stared past her looking out the window.

She cleared the crumpled wads of paper, broken pencils and workbooks out my desk and moved me to the back desk in the far corner of the room to stare at the clock and look out of the window ("all I wanted to," my teacher said.) I watched the snow melt, the puddles grow, gather and drain away, the grass turn from brown to green and counted robins until June.

I did learn to read, of course. The principal found a method she invented using notched cutouts in colored paper rulers. She coached me every morning, all summer. Luckily, I caught up with my reading class by December of my fourth grade and didn't have to suffer the anger and humiliation that my parents would have if I flunked.

Some days, when I felt calm and alert, information came through my senses in an orderly way. The sun didn't glint blindingly, making my stomach hurt. Noises didn't bombard my head causing my brain to overload and short circuit. My skin didn't feel burned all over with my clothing scratching and grating every sensitive pore. On these calm days, thoughts and sensations could be sorted out in an organized way.

Most days, I felt that I was caught in a tumbling, swishing wave; being tossed and turned over and over, hitting bottom, then surfacing to the bright light, loud noises and grating voices which overwhelmed me. I could only catch small snatches of conversation or directions. Often by the time I could decipher, the words were loud and angry. I would feel a slap across my face, coming from, seemingly to me, NOWHERE, connecting to nothing. WHAT? Is all I could say. WHAT? Coming back from my nothing place.

I believe that learning to play the violin at an early age was critical to me since it gave me an access to my emotions without need for words. I could feel emotions through the vibration of the violin strings. The harmonic vibration of a stringed instrument is often soothing to persons with autism. My mother said that even as a small child, whenever I heard a violin play I would run to the couch, climbing up to bounce my head against the cushioned back. She said it was better then hitting my head against the floor. Playing phonograph recordings became a method of distracting me from head banging on hard objects.

I feel that I am coordinated; I like athletics and tumbled exceptionally well as a child. I was chosen to be a mascot for the high school girl's tumbling team when I was eight. I swam with a synchronized team in the summer. We pretended to be, beautiful, graceful, Esther Williams, the great swimmer who starred in Hollywood movies. Except that I didn't know who Esther was at the time, or why this was important to the other kids. I mimicked them by putting my hand behind my head and strutting like they were without a clue to what it was about!

Surprisingly I had many friends, but not friends in the way friendships are usually viewed and how I know now that they can be, with intimacy and caring. I viewed friends as commodities to be manipulated for their toys, pets or interests that we shared. My friends apparently didn't know this, because they would get sad and miss me when I neglected them. Since I could not manage the intensity of a three-way friendship, I had two "close" friends who shared time with me. If we tried to play altogether, we would have terrible fights.

Our parents got together to settle the problem. This became the arrangement: On some days, I played with Janie and another with Carol Lou. Never all three of us! This worked out quite well for me. However, my collections of marbles, rocks, crystal prisms, colored foil, ink pens and smooth buttons were more important to me than my friends. I hid them in my secret place in the attic and would not show them to anyone.

Sewing

I loved the feel of fabric and wanted to learn to sew, but my mother did not know how. My grandmother taught me to sew. She lived in Iowa. I was sent to stay with her for a few weeks to give my parents a break. They told my grandmother that I was probably incorrigible and going to become a juvenile delinquent. Grandmother said that she didn't think any kid was bad at nine years old...children just need some understanding and firm direction. She was a former grade school teacher, valued structure, was stern, but with a kind heart. Unlike my mother and father, she never hit me. I had two aunts living in the same town in Iowa and a cousin my same age.

For the first time, I realized that I had a "place" in a "family", and a sense of belonging. I was valued for who I was, given praise, taught how to contribute and given some unstructured playtime, with a definite beginning and end. We worked, played and ate on a daily schedule.

In answer to my question, grandmother explained that the black contraption sitting underneath the lace covered south windows was an old treadle sewing machine. She was making some bibbed work aprons for my cousin and me to wear in the kitchen. I asked if I could learn to sew. Her "teacher" face lit up. "Yes," she said, "It might be just the trick for you with all of that extra energy that you have, but first you will have to learn how to run it safely."

Some of you may know that a treadle sewing machine is

propelled by rocking both feet in tandem, in an even pace. Stopping and starting requires a coordinated foot movement, using the left foot for a brake. You could stop and then reverse directions by tilting the rocking panel in the opposite way. She told me later, that she didn't think that I could master the difficult procedure but that the energy that it took for me to rock the treadle foot would be good for me. She removed the large needle so that I wouldn't stick myself. The more I rocked the better I got. I practiced every chance I could. One day, my Grandmother placed a size 16 needle in the machine and taught me how to thread it.

Soon, I was cutting out shorts and cut-off tops for my cousin and me to wear. I used old bed sheets and rickrack scraps from grandmother's workbasket. With some trial and error I discovered how much fabric to add for width and length so the garments fit. I asked my aunts what they called someone who makes clothes from their own ideas and they said a dress designer. I remembered the gorgeous clothes hanging neatly on racks in the Cole's Department store in Brookings, and I knew that I wanted to design dresses someday.

My family moved to northern Minnesota where I attended high school. I continued to sew, making skirts and blouses for my mother and sisters as well as for myself, buying patterns and fabric at J.C. Penney's. On some days I held myself stiffly erect, barely moving my head or shoulders for fear that I would crack into a thousand pieces. I spent my free time playing my violin, singing in the church choir, and designing and sewing new clothes for myself. I did not understand boys or date very often.

I attended one year of college at Bemidji University, then left home at 18 to complete an Associate of Arts degree in business at the University of Minnesota. When I was nineteen I got married. We had two daughters. I returned to college when I was much older to complete a four-year degree. I received a Bachelor of Science Degree when I was forty-one. I got divorced shortly after graduating. Two years later, I met my husband, Jay. We are celebrating our tenth anniversary this August!

During my senior year, at the University of Minnesota, a remarkable thing happened! Our Costume Design Department and the Fashion Group of Minneapolis cosponsored a New York City designer, Koos Van Den Akker, to bring his collection to the Twin Cities for a fashion show. Those of us who were seniors in the design program were invited to talk to him about our future careers designing clothing and to show him our portfolios. I stood at the back of the group watching as he looked at the other designers' work. When he looked at mine and asked "Whose is this?"

I stepped forward and introduced myself. He said, "You have talent."

I felt speechless and stared back at him, trying to smile. My teacher Amir Fazali did not believe that I had gifted talent; she had arranged for another student of hers, Karen, to interview for an Apprentice Position with Koos.

Koos studied in and worked at the house of Christian Dior in Paris. He is of Dutch origin and is known for his unusual combinations of texture and color in the clothing that he designs. I admired his collection and asked if I could come to New York to just to see his studio workroom. Surprisingly, he said "Yes, bring your portfolio." After I showed Koos my garments and artwork, he said he liked my sewing and surprised me by offering me an apprenticeship with him for the fall collection. I felt very lucky to be asked. I inquired if he thought I was Karen, the person Miss Fazali had spoken about to him.

He said, "Who is Karen? I want you to work for me. You can sew. Where did you learn the European techniques?"

"My Grandmother taught me, and by studying couture sewing books."

I worked for several weeks under his tutelage. Riding the subway to his Seventh Avenue Studio was one of the most difficult parts of living in New York City, because of the odors, crowds and noise.

Sensory

My sensory system is very easily overstimulated. I am sensitive to bright light, noise and rough textures. I have learned to meditate to lower my anxiety level. I have meditated most of my life. When I was four years old, a Zen priest was visiting my neighbor, Dr. Chistopherson, who was a philosopher. The Zen priest took an interest in me and my curiosity about his strange brown robes. He showed me how to sit in meditation, and to breathe deeply that summer.

It is helpful to meditate to reduce stress. When I feel the stress, I feel jittery in my body. I may appear calm on the outside, but, often, I am shaking on the inside. I heard a wonderful description of this feeling from a meditation teacher who shows mothers with low incomes how to breath deeply, meditate and thereby reduce stress. She calls this meditation "Settling down the static in your attic!" Static in the attic! Static describes the fuzziness I feel in my head!

There are several ways that I can reduce my static. I take Calmplex, which is a homeopathic remedy, it is very mild so my nervous system can tolerate it. I can sleep through most of the night now and do not have night terrors, which are frightening random images from which I cannot awaken. I also take vitamins, DMG (N-Di methyl glycine), Magnesium with Vitamins B-6 and C. Each person's nutritional needs are different. What may be helpful to me may not be beneficial for someone else.

This past fall I saw a physical therapist to learn about sensory integration. The therapist created a "diet" for me to use whenever I want to calm down or "calm up" (to raise my energy level). Diet is the terminology used by a physical therapist for a program designed to help with sensory integration. My diet includes jumping on a small trampoline several times a day; I use a small brush and a prescribed method to brush my skin, which calms my sensitivity to touch. The trampoline tends to energize me, and I feel more clear thinking. Rocking in a chair is relaxing as well as swinging. I like to take long walks, which helps release toxins in my muscles and feels energizing mentally and physically.

Usually, I have a warning if I am becoming overloaded with too much stimuli. I get crabby, am controlling and feel weak or sleepy. My thought process slows down. Now that I am more aware of my energy levels, I can better regulate the way I feel. Some other ways I take care of myself are to have more variety in the things I eat. Foods that require more chewing and are spicy help me develop a wider tolerance. I like to avoid hard surfaced rooms with florescent lighting. The flickering often causes me pain. Florescent light also affects my ability to decipher sound. It isn't my hearing ears that are the problem, but my ability to decipher what I am hearing, to make sense out of the sounds. I do not like applause. The random sound is painful for me. This is the reason that I have asked that you refrain from applause.

As I said, I never wanted to be different, I just was. At some level, I knew that I couldn't fit in. Many times, when I was growing up, I felt like I was rushing to catch up as if I were the last to join a spiral folk dance that was undulating out of control, always running, and out of breath. I have come to accept that I am the way I am, I cannot change this.. that I am autistic. Some things may not be possible to change, and this could be one of them. My feeling is that we can put our best efforts to the task of understanding and discovery, but that sometimes things cannot be changed.

However, and this is my hope for you today, I believe that I can change how autism impacts my life and those near to me by the way that I choose to respond. Sometimes the choice is difficult, and perhaps for some, not possible. But those of us who can change the way in which we respond, by giving our best effort to make things better, then letting go and living our lives in acceptance, transform negative energy into positive! The key to acceptance is to accept for now...just for now. Tomorrow, next week, next year could be different. But for now live fully.

Many of the stories I am telling you today were repeated over and over by my Mother, as if she wanted me to give her some sort of explanation for my behavior. I know she felt that she had failed me as a mother. On one of the last visits we had before she died of cancer fourteen years ago, Mother said that she felt sad that she hadn't been a very good parent for me. She said that she was sorry for the way she tried to parent me, that she just didn't know what to do, that she just never understood me.

I'm relieved that we had this conversation. It laid to rest my deepest wish that our relationship could have been different. Some things just are.

You may be disappointed that I have not prepared a list of what to do, how to do it and which treatments are best. This is something that I cannot deliver for you. I do not have the answers. I can suggest that you join or start a parent support group in your area. Parents I've talked to, said that many times they found that the support they received from other parents, that talking about their child with autism to someone who understood, was essential to their sanity. They discovered people who knew how difficult it is to parent a child, or in some cases, several children with special needs.

In Conclusion

I believe that each of us can contribute in the search for answers to the profoundly mysterious nature of autism. That sometimes a window will open in a wall that we could not see before--a window to see out, onto a clear day of understanding.

I want to read a short poem by the great Sufi poet, Rumi, and ask if you would kindly refrain from applause.

I've chosen a flower as a visual image to leave with you. In the Spring, the woodland Trillium rises up from the sun-warmed soil. I look for signs of it underneath the oak trees of our nature center. At first the Trillium appears as a green leaf that looks somewhat like a blade of grass. When the conditions are favorable it bursts forth unfolding into a radiant flower of purest white. It represents a symbol of hope for me...hope that each person affected by autism can

Ruth Elaine Hane

rise to their fullest potential.

(Rumi)
The human form is a ghost
Made of distraction and pain
Sometimes
pure light
Sometimes cruel
Trying wildly to open
this image held tightly within itself.

About the Author

Ruth Elaine recounts with vivid memory stories of her life that, in retrospect, are characteristics of profound early autism, giving others a glimpse into what was like to be lost in her nothing world. She offers hope to others affected by this baffling disorder

Ruth Elaine Hane, BS, Human Ecology, University of Minnesota, Magna cum laude, Phi Beta Kappa, Reiki Master/ Teacher. MidWest Director, Autism Society of America, ASA Board of Director Candidate Review Committee, Autism Tract Committee, Conference Committee, Co-facilitator, ASA TownMeeting, Past Vice President, Autism Society of Minnesota. Ruth Elaine is a frequent panel participant and speaker. She is writing chapters for two books on autism and her Memoir. Married, with four children, she lives in Minneapolis with her husband, Jay, and three cats.

Diagnosed with High Functioning Autism in 1995, Ruth Elaine volunteers as a consultant to parents, teens, young adults, professionals, and caregivers. She established Teen Get-Together and Adult Get-Together: social groups for teens and adults on the Autism Spectrum.

She helps sensitive people thrive through strategies for

stress reduction. Ruth Elaine volunteers at Pathways, a center for people affected by a health crisis and at North Memorial Hospital, Residence Hospice.

Contact Ruth at ruthelaine.hane@gmail.com

Sandra visits her symbol of freedom in New York City

Sandra Radisch
Sandra: The Sometimes Invisible Woman

Originally presented at TASH 2001

My name is Sandra Radisch and I have autism. I am bright. I am talented. I have hopes and dreams. I have problems.

I would like to begin by saying it's mighty hard to live without a voice. I have lived my life in silence, and I'll be damned if some professionals are going to lock me up again.

My voice does not work properly. It is not under my control. I cannot say what I want to say when I want to. Sometimes words just pop out when I don't want them to. Only with extreme effort can I say what I mean to say, and then I am limited to a few phrases like *"sugar please"* or *"coffee please."*

All the tests I was given were used to describe what I couldn't do. Limits were set by others, and I learned to believe them, even though I knew I was capable in my mind. I happen to have a body that does not perform in accordance with my mind's command, so I cannot demonstrate competence. Sometimes I get stuck and can't get started again. My muscles don't remember how to move or something. I believe I will improve my movements.

I want to have my story read by professionals and by the public at large. Professionals need to hear from those of us with autism and those of us with the supposed label of retardation. I really also want to reach those who only know what they see on TV. I want my story to be helpful to people who support people with autism, like parents and direct contact staff. Also, I want my story to support Facilitated Communication (FC) and possibly to entertain, because I am pretty strange.

My first memory is as a baby, more than one, less than two. My memory is of crying in my mother's arms and not wanting to be held. I did not like to be held because my mother smelled too strongly of perfume. It made my head swim. I don't have that reaction now. In fact, I like to wear perfume myself .

Going to school was a disappointment. I could not figure out why I was excluded. I did not think I was so weird. I was thrown out of school after two hours – forever. I think I was excluded because I could not speak. I'm still confused why my speech or my voice betrayed me. At sometime early on I stopped being able to get words out when I wanted to. When I understood I was never going to speak normally, I wished I had not been born. Never in a million years did I dream I would be able to communicate for myself before FC.

As a child I was caught up in my obsessions most of the time, but I was interested in the world, too. The thing is, it is hard to remember how or what I thought about as a child. I remember listening to my brothers and sister doing their homework and thinking about the material, whatever it was. I do know that I heard about science.

I knew I was smart when I understood the homework my brothers and sister did for school. Mom made them do their homework at the dining room table. Sometimes they asked questions of mom or each other, and I knew the right answer. I listened and learned. I don't want to suggest that I got a full education or that I always paid full attention, but I got a lot more than my family would have guessed or believed...and more than the specialists said I would or ever could..

My family valued science and math, and my sister Marilyn loved Shakespeare. My brother Burt liked to make models of airplanes. He was interested in flying and talked a lot about the science of it, like lift, weight of fuel, and speed. Mach 3 was a record for a while for somebody.

Growing up I did a lot of the usual "autistic" stuff. I have always loved thinking about how the world works. My favorite pastime was my toilet experiments. I had a curiosity about where things went when you flush the toilet. I necessarily needed many trials, and I never figured out where the stuff went. My friend Carolyn explained it to me a while ago. When I couldn't figure it out myself, I changed the experiment to how much I could send away in a single flush. You would be surprised what water can move—soap bars, wash cloths, sponges, after shave bottles, paper, but never toothbrushes or tubes of paste (too long for the hole). I tried some objects many times before I gave up.

My father became skilled in plumbing. Mom got yelled at by dad for my failed attempts because he had to take the toilet apart to unclog it. My success were gone for good and underreported to dad for obvious reasons. Finally I quit because mom and dad would fight over it, and it was both upsetting and unfair. He would say to watch me more, but I was too quick and mom was too busy. He held her more responsible than me, and even I knew that wasn't fair. I still like to flush the toilet whenever I can because I like to see the water swirl, and frankly, it has become a habit.

Another fascination I had was about the lights in the house. Sometimes when I flicked the light switch it would make a different kind of sound. Was it caused by a change in my touch or was it something else? I never figured it out, and it became an obsession or a habit, not science.

I was hyperactive as a child as soon as I could walk. I had a habitual interest in rooftops. Up there I felt free, on my own, on top of the world, but I scared mom to death. I moved very quickly and ran around the house like a blur. I made mom chase me all over the house. Mom said I was like a tornado, whatever that is. I got out of sight in an instant. She usually found me by the sound of water, running or flushing or both. I was my father's little Angel who didn't know any better. So when I did something wrong, mom was accused of not watching me closely enough, as if that were possible.

As I got older, I spent a lot of time sitting. Mom let me because at least I was not getting into trouble. The older I got, the more happy I was to just sit. Dad hated that. Forcing me to get off the couch was his main concern. He made me get up, and we took long walks. He walked, I didn't. He had to pull me along, especially as I got older.

Walks with dad are one of my favorite memories. He loved nature. Dad always wanted me to see wonder-filled nature, the flowers and birds. We walked, partly looking at the world, but also for exercise. He'd talk about the beauty around us here, and the importance of the health of the body and mind. My dad loved the garden far more than mom. He had roses of many colors. I don't think he had any favorite color, but he liked to tend them. He fed them and cut them. I often sat outside with him because he believed fresh air was good for you.

Dad has always given me hope because he was patient and kind. He was always soft- spoken. He was the one to say, "She's just a child. Maybe she's sick." He excused my behavior. Dad never yelled at me, but everyone else did—especially mom. I hastened to make mom mad. Her temper was shorter than the flush of a toilet. I liked to slam doors. I broke toys by throwing them, like my brother's models.

My sister Carol gives me sorrow. She was the youngest,

and I made her cry a lot. She wished we could play together, but mom told her my play was different. She played the piano. I played with toilets and light switches. My mom was beside herself when Carol was little. I would be loud. Carol would cry. Mom would yell. Mom would cry, and I would just run around. I liked Carol, but I just couldn't stop.

My behavior got out of control in adolescence. Carol hated my lack of control. She just wanted a normal family. She screamed it loudly quite often. Mom asked her to think what if it was her instead. She was just a kid, but she asked good questions like, "Why does she run and not get punished like me?"

I understood their frustrations, but no one could imagine mine. I was 16. I saw no future in sight, so I began my reign of terror. I became hell on wheels. I bit myself and had quite a temper. Who was in more despair—my mom, my dad, my sister and brothers, or poor, retarded, autistic Sandra? I finally acted mine out. To all it was horror.

I broke a plate glass window with my head, so, in an attempt to keep me safe, I was sent to Napa State Hospital for the insane. I went to Napa dying to know why I couldn't be like normal people. I heard I was autistic from family and doctors, but I thought that meant stupid/retarded. I knew I was not stupid, so I thought I was not autistic. I wanted them to find out what was wrong with me and fix it. I bit my wrist a lot and was furious all the time. It was either shut out the world or bite. I was putting my life on the line with crazy behaviors to get my mom or dad to get me some help.

I wanted help but did not expect to be sent away. Mom and dad did not explain it to me. I did know mom was packing some of my stuff, but I didn't understand I was going to live elsewhere until they left me and my bags on the ward that was to be my home for years.

There was a ward for us retards on a floor by ourselves. I looked out the small window of the door at my fellow prisoners in the hall, wondering how long I would have to stay locked up like that. Of course life was a nightmare. On top of autism there was abuse, failure, blame, and a denial of my humanity.

I loved time out. It was the only time I ultimately was alone in a quiet place. One had to be careful not to act out too much, or you were drugged out. I earned going to time out by jumping up and down and biting my wrist and hitting myself on the legs. I informed the staff in autism by flushing things down the toilet for the first time in years.

I did not like the ward, and I finally understood I had to shape up to get out, so I did. It was a waste of time to B. [behavior] Manage me, especially given my love of time out. Hope lived outside the locked door. I wanted OUT, but what came next was worse by far.

I was moved to what was called a group home, but I called it hell on earth. I lived in a shack in back of the house they showed mom. I rarely bathed, never brushed my teeth, and ate slop from a bowl without utensils. They kept mom away, saying I needed time to adjust. I lost a lot of weight.

They were grossed out by me, or so they said. They were more cruel by neglect than abuse. Try to picture a movie with a POW camp. I had walls, not bars like GI Jane. They did not beat me up except with words. I do not remember seeing others with disabilities, but there may have been others there. Obviously, when Mom was finally allowed to see me, she immediately took me out of there. Ultimately, she and a group of other parents made plans to open a group home, where I continue to live today.

Adulthood

When I first moved into the group home formed by my parents, I was afraid to trust anyone, and I was largely ignored. I either sat on the couch or laid on my bed. I got very little attention unless I bit my wrist. My mom and the team made up my goals like my behavior plan, which was stupid. I got a reward for not biting all day. I think I got coffee if I didn't bite all day. What a laugh.

I went to a day program. I did not enjoy my group, which was total care people mostly. By this I mean people who needed diapers changed or did not feed themselves. I guess I was in there because I also wet myself sometimes, so I guess we were the toileting group. That is mostly what was going on. Sometimes there was some face washing. Hygiene was apparently important.

I sat and rocked a lot. I did not have much to think about or look forward to, so I don't know how I tolerated it. I was younger then, and did not hope or expect much. A good day was defined by whether I stayed dry. I felt mostly invisible but nicely more capable than the rest of my group.

I wished I had a normal body or at least a voice so I could really get a life. My life then was wait, clean up, wait, bite a little, clean up, wait, rock a little, clean up, and get on the bus. Until 1992, I could only communicate that I wanted or needed something by biting my wrist. Everyone had to guess what I needed. Many times they guessed right...but so many times they guessed wrong. I screamed inside for a way to express my needs, desires, thoughts and feeling. Then they tried facilitated communication with me. Here's the deal. A person gives my hand resistance while I point to letters to spell words. My facilitator never moves my hand for me. They pull back on my hand while I push forward. This has helped me concentrate and it has made my hand stronger. The first time I typed, everyone realized that I was not as stupid as they thought.

My first words were welcomed by all. My mom was so happy she cried. At first I got everything I asked for. It was easy because I asked for simple things, like a cup of hot tea after my bath. But as time went by, it got more complicated. My mom was so used to speaking and deciding for me that it took a long time for her to adjust and remember to ask me first. She struggled with letting go of the controls. I was afraid to disagree with her for a long time, too. I had a lot to learn, a lot to catch up on.

A few years ago I led some self-advocacy groups for my peers. I taught self-advocacy. It's funny that I should be teaching others to speak up for themselves because my communication is not so free. Typing is very slow, and sometimes, while I am typing, other people keep talking... leaving me behind. I can't really interrupt or yell at somebody or make spontaneous comments like you folks who speak. I am working hard toward independent typing, but for now I need someone to help me. Without a facilitator I am plunged back into silence and invisibility. I wanted to learn about self-advocacy and to teach others because there must be many others like myself who are still trying to find their voice and still struggling to have it be heard.

When I was younger, I was tolerant, I think, because I could get more lost in an obsession. I ignored whatever was going on around me with ease. For example, I may not have heard someone enter the room if I was flicking a light switch when I was little. Now the only activity that continues to hold my attention is water play. I make spectacular water fountains with my hands under water. None of my "normal" friends have come even close to my display. I can also get swept away in classical or good jazz music.

I used to be more isolated in my own world. When I began using FC, several things changed. For one, people talked to me more and explained things, so I paid more attention to what people said and did, how things worked and stuff. Before FC I guessed about stuff like why the world works the way it does. I was surprised by how much I had wrong. I was surprised by how much I had right. I am sad that, even now, people don't tend to talk to me because I can't talk back. You can't imagine how it feels to have people talk about you, around you, for you, when you are standing right there. I appear and disappear many times during a day.

I have always been stubborn. As long as I can remember, I've usually done what I've wanted or what my body would allow. When I was younger, as I told you, I had more energy. I moved all the time. What I do not know is this: Did I have more control? I've had more trouble getting started with each passing year. When I was little, I ran around a lot. Did I run where I wanted to or did I just eventually get there (faster)?

I think I had more control, or maybe I had less automatic movement. Automatic movements are the things you can do without thinking about them, like undressing. Automatic movement patterns are vastly overrated. Rather than helping me get through the day, they are the enemy. Maybe I just want/need to change my shirt, but the next thing you know, I am completely undressed, because it is automatic.

I have several different problems with movements. Sometimes I can't get started. In my mind I think, "I want to go to my room," but the message doesn't get to my legs. I am frozen and can't get up by myself. Sometimes I can move when someone gives me an instruction, but sometimes I can't move until I am touched. That is bad enough, but also, sometimes I can't stop moving. I call this my "fiddles." I do not remember fiddles as a child. Compulsions, yes, fiddles, no. It might start out because my glasses slip down on my nose and I actually manage to push them back up. But then I don't stop. What was a useful movement explodes into a full blown fiddle, and I push my glasses up so many times that my nose gets red unless someone helps me stop.

I have a hard time switching and combining movements. I have very little control over my body a lot of the time, and that is very frustrating.

I have told you that I can say some words. Most are just echoes of things I have heard that make no sense in the moment. The words just pop out. It annoys me as much as my staff. If my emotions are under control, so is my voice. Emotions unexpressed are stronger, plus I am very sensitive.

I must feel things more intensely because I do bite over the smallest thing. I am pleased when my body matches my emotions. It doesn't happen all that often, almost never when sad. I did not cry when my father or my mother died. The grief and pain went on and on. If only I could have cried. In movies, it looks like such a relief to cry. Happiness is easier. It sometimes explodes out in laughter and jumping. When I am comfortable, it is fairly easy to smile. Frustration, anger, disappointment become biting and the occasional wry smile. This is the limit of bodily expression of my feelings. Pathetic.

I am very sensitive to others. For example, when others are upset, I'm upset. When my sister Carol was upset, I bit, and when my housemates are upset, I bite if I can't get away. It is not just the noise, which of course is hard to take. I feel sorry for the person who is upset. I do not remember when I became sensitive to others' feelings, but I was fairly young. That's not to say I always know or interpret others' feelings correctly. I am often wrong about that. It bothers me to see others unhappy, especially if they do not speak—babies and us.

I now care what others think of me. As a child, I could not have cared less, even when the doctors said I did not have a prayer for a normal life. Now I am also interested in how people's minds work. Remember, I said before that I was not as aware that I was so different when I was young. Now I am fascinated by others' opinions, perceptions and stuff.

Before FC I thought I had a lot figured out. What I did not realize is that I made a lot of incorrect assumptions. I just did my best to understand what I saw and experienced. For example, I thought my body was mostly like everyone else's in terms of how I sense things, but I found out that I could hear better than most people. My mom heard about auditory training and said maybe I should try it. She noticed, correctly, that I became upset when I heard some sounds, like the vacuum cleaner. She told me a story about a girl who started to talk after having her hearing corrected. To tell the truth, I was disappointed with the results. I thought auditory training would cure me. When all was said and done, my hearing was better, but nothing else was remarkable. I could not screen out the important from the unimportant. Since auditory training, I do not have that problem, but sudden noises still really bother me.

Keep in mind I am autistic, so I may have very different perceptions about people's expectations, like why is eye contact so important? I wish I had a dollar for each time somebody told me to look at them. I see best when I look out of the corner of my eye. If you make me look at you, I can't necessarily see you well.

I am often torn between wanting to pass as normal and really preferring some tolerance and acceptance, for I totally believe the world must learn to celebrate diversity, not fear it. I know I must compromise some. I can't pull my pants down outside the bathroom at the mall. I have to wait until I get inside, no matter what. I can't pop out with, "Damn you, Will," at the ballet just because I am nervous. But I should be allowed to be different from the norm. Can't you all stretch just a little? Maybe I should move to New York City where no one even looked, much less stared at me.

One year I went to visit New York City after speaking at a FC conference. The day we first saw Lady Liberty (Statue of Liberty), the sun was bright and you could see her from afar. Understand that I had little hope for freedom and none for liberty. She offered, yes, begged for all people to be free. This included me. From this introduction to her, I got to thinking. I, too, want liberty for bitter people like me who never even dreamed the dream to be in control of my life beyond little daily choices or my goals for next year. Before FC, I lived in fear like all those who must depend on others to fulfill their needs. I so much wanted for them to see inside. I so much wanted people to give me choices rather than demands. My inside self and my outside self are very different. No one would have known this without FC. The statue of liberty has become my personal symbol of freedom .

I want to talk a little more about FC. In the beginning it was like a rescue from a cave-in. Suddenly the outside world heard my call! I am here! I would not have had this opportunity if my mom had not insisted. For all her frustration and irritation, she knew I was more intelligent than the label of profound retardation that they gave me. When I was a child, I did clever things, like walking on the roof. After the first time the firemen got me down from the roof, my Dad started installing clever latches and locks. Although I was labeled profoundly retarded, I figured each one out in time. Mom saw this sort of stuff and knew that more was going on inside me than others gave me credit for. My poor body no longer performs the feats that awarded me this status.

FC changed everything for me because people could finally see that the outside me and the inside me did not agree. This has been hard over the years for people to understand and support.

At first I spelled words the way they sounded to my ear. Carolyn taught me to spell and to use punctuation and grammar rules.

In the beginning, I call it the "golden years," Carolyn and the Speech Pathologist taught all the staff at home and at day program to facilitate. At first I just made requests and daily choices but, in time, I became the center of my team; sometimes, I was the leader. Whenever someone talked to me, they had a letter board or a typing device in their hands. They expected me to have something to say all the time. I made whole phrase boards for the things I could predict I wanted to say during routine tasks, from personal care to planning my activities. Whole word phrase boards were quicker and easier than typing out each word, and the targets were bigger, so I could point with less support.

The decline of the golden years was gradual. It began with the anti-FC TV shows, like Frontline. Lines were being drawn, and some professionals quit my team. As staff turned over in my day program and at home, there was less and less belief in my competence. Over the years I had at least one or two staff I could type with. Although I could use my phrase boards with even the newest staff, they were gradually used less and less. And, of course, I could never go get the board for myself. The fatal blow came when my friend Carolyn quit her job as the director of my group home. The staff that were trained "bothered" only occasionally, and the new staff were never trained. It was more or less the same at my day program. Now I still type with Carolyn, but my team is questioning if I can communicate at all. It doesn't matter to them if I have validated my typing by telling Carolyn something that she did not already know but could confirm as fact through someone else.

I am painfully aware that the organizations that support me determine everything about my voice. Do I get to communicate at all? Will they teach the staff to facilitate? How many staff? On what shift? The staff decides how often or much I need to talk. How often am I given a voice? Of equal concern is whether my voice will be heard. Will anyone act on my communication? I have always been dependent on staff for things like taking a bath or brushing my teeth. Other people would complain if I had bad breath or bad body odor, but who can I count on to complain if I am silenced? This dependence is very new and frightening to me. You can't imagine the emotional torment ranging from rage and frustration to despair and hopelessness.

Before FC people did not talk to me much or explain things to me. After FC everything was described and explained. My opinions were sought and valued. Before doctors' appointments I typed out questions for them. The doctors asked me questions rather than asking my staff, and I could answer with FC. My mother thought I had a seizure the day I moved into the group home. For many years I took medicine to prevent seizures. I am the one who convinced the doctor that I did not need the medicine. The medicine was discontinued, and I never had another seizure. Now if Carolyn can go to the appointment with me, she does, but if she can't, I have no way of reporting what I feel.

Before FC people said all kind of things in front of me. Staff gossiped. They described sex with their boyfriends or fights with their kids— all kinds of crazy stuff, thinking I did not understand. Oh boy! The stories I could tell! After FC those who believed in my intelligence would be more careful about what they said in front of me. Early on, when I first started typing, a new staff person, Gaby, was talking about her trip to Hawaii. Carolyn was not there at the time, but when she came to work, I typed "Tell Gaby to take me with her to Hawaii next time." Gaby was instantly convinced I could type my own thoughts. She told everybody the story, and they all began to censor what they said around me. Less fun, but more respect! Now most people again say all kinds of stuff in front of me, thinking—what? I don't understand? I am not listening? I can't tell anyone what I hear? The worst is when they say stuff about me that is not true. That convinces me that they do not see me as being competent, as being able to communicate or being valuable. It makes me feel mad and vulnerable and afraid. I call myself the incredible invisible woman. It is not a trick I do myself. It is a trick that is played on me by other people. I want to end with a poem I wrote about it.

Now you see me, Now you don't
I haven't changed
You have
I will give you words to take to heart
I am and always will be
Right here
Waiting to be seen again

About the Author

Sandra is 50 something, and she lives in Northern California. She enjoys writing and never passes up an opportunity for public speaking. She can be reached at **csnuyens@comcast.net** or PO Box 429, Forest Knolls, California 94933. She welcomes your comments or questions.

Nick Pentzell
3 Presentations

This (untitled) essay and the one that follows were
presented at the 2002 Everyday Lives Convention,
"Making It Happen," in Hershey, Pennsylvania,
as part of a panel of facilitated communication users,
"The Lonesome Doves: Our Journey"

Most of you live in bodies that do what your brain tells them
to do. I don't. I command, I ask, I wheedle, I plead, and
sometimes my body responds, but sometimes it doesn't, or it
makes clumsy, ill-directed attempts to do my bidding. I send
out directions as if they were the lost and windblown letters
of an inept skywriter, and I take in information all at once, like
a hand calculator trying to add, subtract, multiply, and divide
all at once while computing Einstein's Theory of Relativity. My
circuits often fry in overload. As a small child, I was poorly
equipped to deal with the frustration of a miscreant body, and

I coped by cushioning myself from stimulus in a spaced-out world, or else by speeding up my intake of stimulation until I exploded in a delightful burst of fierce emotion. My thinking was a passing array of disordered images, with the sounds of a word thrown in here and there: "da," "ma," "balloo," and the handful of other sounds I could then speak, as well as words or phrases I heard or saw on TV. The world seemed chaotic and arbitrary. I seemed chaotic, but I did not want to be arbitrary!

When I was thirteen, the speech teacher in the Severely Mentally Impaired classroom (where I was unfortunately placed) taught me facilitated communication. I surprised everyone by spelling words and demonstrating my intelligence. Within a year I was an inclusion student in the public school system, where I attended from fifth grade to eleventh, taking required academic courses, but with study halls instead of electives. In eleventh grade, I began sitting in on college classes, and I decided to continue auditing classes at the college level, taking courses in philosophy and literature, instead of finishing high school. I plan to get my GED in the near future, then work on a college degree.

In the past year I have joined the Lonesome Doves and become a board member of Autism Living and Working, a group of autistic people and their parents who are trying to legislate an Autism Waiver in Pennsylvania so that adults disabled by autism can receive funding to live independently (with support) in their communities. I have gone to Harrisburg to talk with state officials and legislative aides; it is a powerful thing to be able to work directly to change my life and to better the lives of others like me who may not have a voice.

Before I learned facilitated communication, my existence inside my body was a kind of frustrating hell. Now that I can communicate, much of my frustration with processing information can be worked through, because I have the words to explain what is happening to me. I also can do and experience so much more than I could before. But the greatest thing that has happened is that I am able to more truly be Myself.

Everybody else sees me as emerging from within, but I had to find myself before I was capable of coming out. Because of facilitated communication, I was able to recognize myself as the Thinker in my brain, instead of seeing myself as the victim of fears and impulses. This was not easy. My development of a solid Self has taken time and effort, yet I don't think it could have happened without language.

I must explain that words are my power. Yes, I can tell people what I want, but I can also feed my creativity and intelligence. I am not stuck in a loop of infantile desires. I am not so dependent on other people to make sense for me of a world that used to appear erratic and random. I am so Me, so far from the fearful soul I used to be, hiding inside my uncooperative body. With language I can comprehend life, I can explain concepts that are beyond the limitations of my mind-pictures.

My life of action is something I love; I want to experience more and more. This would be a hollow shell if I were not in control of the Me within. Chaos lurks in the recesses, but I am armed with the words I need to turn it into order.

Introduction to FC

Facilitated communication (FC) is a means of providing support and sensory input to people who have movement disoders, enabling them to communicate by pointing to a keyboard. The concept can be applied to other activities as well. I have used FC to move game pieces, to draw and write, and to play a drum. Any activity that requires hand movement can be facilitated, in principle.

There are several points to consider before attempting FC with a disabled person.

- Make sure the person knows you and is comfortable with you. I often go for a walk with a new facilitator before we begin FC, so I can learn how the facilitator reacts to me.
- Be sure the person wants to communicate with you. Ask.

- Treat him or her with respect, as an intellectual equal. Assume competence.
- Take time to become comfortabe touching hands. Many people who respond to FC are hypersensitive to touch.

The concept of FC is simple, but mastering it can be hard. Basically, the facilitator offers strong resistance to the wobbling of the person's hand. Think of pulling upwards and back, towards the person. **Resistance** is something I cannot stress enough. I never receive enough from a new facilitator. Make the person push against you as if your hand was a lever. (Once you are comfortable facilitating, you can probably fade back the pressure, but at the beginning, strong resistance will make the person's physical signals clear. You will also provide a firm support so the person feels he or she is in control and not foundering.)

To begin

If you can, find out if the person is right- or lefthanded. Ask if she or he has a preference.

I suggest establishing clear "yes" and "no" signals. If traditional nodding and shaking of the head are not something the person can do, or if the person cannot signal unaided, create signals the person can easily do with facilitation. I touch my head for "yes" and my stomach for "no" and require only a light touch on my arm to do this.

This gives you a way to communicate and get feedback when you are ready to do finer movements on a keyboard. It also gives you a preview of FC, since you will feel the person inititiate movement.

Take the person's hand with your strongest hand. Most people respond well to pressure at the palm, at least in the beginning. Some people also require help isolating their index fingers.

Pull up and back, towards the person, and away from the keyboard. Return to this pull back position after every letter. Try typing something both of you know, like the person's name.

Ask the person to tap the first letter. Keep up resistant pressure until the person's finger touches the key. If you lose the feel of the person's push, return to the pull back position. Adjust for side to side or twisting movements.

Many people require letter by letter feedback at first, or in situations where focusing is difficult. Say each letter aloud to validate correct facilitating (or set a talking device to letter by letter readback). I now prefer readback at the end of a sentence, but I find that new listeners who are not familiar with FC interact more with me if I use letter by letter readback. (Too often people ask me a question, then continue talking or walk away before I finish typing.)

Other tips

I find it frustrating to work with new people. Try in brief episodes if FC doesn't come easily. But keep trying, and don't interpret frustration as rejection or inability! With some facilitators, I have begun FCing in two sessions, while others have taken a month or more. It is not so much a matter of personal feeling but a team trust, physical compatibility, and coordination issue.

Games can be a good FC exercise, where the facilitator offers hand resistance while the person moves a game piece. I liked playing Trouble when I was a kid; now I use Connect Four or Chinese Checkers (with pegs) as FC practice.

Use FC everywhere. A person needs to have the option to communicate all the time. Coat a letterboard in plastic so it can be wiped off when used at meals. Take a board on walks, to the store. FC while sitting, walking, rolling on the floor. The technology is less important than the opportunity to participate. Combine paper or cardboard letter boards with computers, talking keyboards like Links or Lightwriters, and touch-operated recorded message devices. Just encourage the person to be expressive, to comment, joke, and be involved!

As soon as you get clear responses and the person can accurately type, start fading back support. The ultimate goal is independence.

Move support to the wrist, forearm, elbow, shoulder—wherever the person can still type accurately. It might take years to achieve, but always keep this goal in mind.

Practice fading back when the person is not tired, stressed, or having to deal with a lot of outside stimulus. For instance, decide whether fading practice is more important than getting schoolwork done or participating in a conversation.

This (untitled) essay was presented in 2003 at the Germantown YWCA in Philadephia, Pennsylvania, at an after-school program for grade-school children, as part of a workshop sponsored by Networks for Training and Development, "Kids Helping Kids ... Learning Together to Be Tolerant, Understanding, & Accepting of Others"

Hey, what are you going to do when you meet a nerdy guy like me who wants to fit in, but whose body grooves to the beat of a different, wild-handed drummer? Snicker? Call him names behind his back? Act like he's invisible? Be nice in an "I feel sorry for you" way?

Heck, no! You know how that makes you feel—about as worthwhile as old chewing gum someone stuck on the underside of your desk. But it IS awkward being around someone who is disabled. So how do you act?

I'll give you some pointers. Assume the person is just like you, but his or her body doesn't work in the same way. Use your eyes more than you do with other people, in order to observe how the person's body behaves, and how the person communicates. I tend to either get excited or nervous when people talk to me. When excited, I get hyper and sometimes I pull away. If this happened, you would probably think I didn't want to talk to you, right? Wrong! I am thrilled, but I just need to move away so that I can reduce my level of contact until I relax. Keep me included in your conversation, and I'll drift back into the group. Other times I freeze up and get stiff; my face won't smile. I feel like I will never be able to please anyone, so I hide inside my body. You can probably melt me by joking around. I'm not saying that all disabled people will react the way I do, but this is the sort of thing to look for.

Please, please, please don't ask dumb questions like, "How old are you? What foods do you like? What's your favorite color?" Talk about the same stuff you do with everybody else. Don't make up fake conversation. It makes a person feel like a fake friend. And—think a minute—if you were a person with speech problems, and it took a lot of time and effort to speak or spell out your words, would you want to put a lot of time and effort into answering these questions? I, for one, would rather gossip, or talk about what's happening at school, in my life, or in the world.

Now, how should you act around a person who has a disability? Should you look away if I'm hitting myself, or eating sloppily, or making weird noises? I mean, you don't want to be rude, right? My own preference is that you continue looking at me, but try not to be fazed by my behavior. I'm trying to do the best I can. I must say that I always have appreciated it when friends have defended me from jerks who think it's funny to pick on people who are different. But with your own friends who are disabled, you might want to overlook the disability until you know them well enough to ask them how they want you to behave around them. It's not rude to ask, or to admit that the situation is awkward. Believe me, the disabled person knows it is uncomfortable, and she or he might feel better if you bring it up.

Again, once you know us as individuals, you can ask us if we want to talk about our disabilites. Many of us don't mind explaining, because we know that the better you understand us, the better you can know us. The surface that you see is merely the wrapped box that conceals the gift of who we are. But we don't want to feel as if, in your eyes, our disabilities define who we are. And just because a person is disabled doesn't mean she or he wants to serve as a spokesperson for Disability In General. I had a teacher in high school who, on the first day of a class called "Disability in Literature," put me on the spot in front of everybody by asking me to tell the class what it felt like to be disabled. She meant well and wanted to offer me a chance to share my experience with the class, but she ended up embarrassing me by drawing my disabled state to the attention of a group of students I'd just met. I'm sure that I'd have been comfortable talking to the class if the teacher had asked me ahead of time if I wanted to, and had waited until the students knew me better, and had given me time to think about and prepare what I wanted to say. A lot of it comes down to the Golden Rule: treat others the way you want them to treat you.

About the Author

In one of my presentations published here, I wrote an autobiographical piece about how my life essentially began in earnest when I was introduced to facilitated communication. Before FC, I had a life of stimulation and sensation, of impulses and desires, of feelings and relationships, of images and flashes of meaning, but it was not a coherent experience of living. Who I am is who I have become through my use of language.

At the time of this printing, I am twenty-five years old and live in suburban Philadelphia. I am a student at a community college, and I plan to transfer to Temple University to complete my B.A. in English before I pursue a Master's degree that will enable me to work in the field of primate communication. I am participating in a pilot program for adults with autism which has a goal of enabling us to live lives of supported independence as active citizens in our communities, and I am also involved with advocacy groups.

More central to my self is my poetry, which I have begun publishing in small journals. It is important to me that I establish myself as a poet on the artistic merits of my work. I write poetry to express my humanity, not my disability. Many essays I have written are pieces that share my experience as a disabled person, but I believe that we must become recognized in areas that are not disability-related if we are to become truly equal to able-bodied people.

Contact Nick at nickpen@juno.com

Barbara Moran

Life in the "Best" Hospital

Parts of this presentation were presented at the
2002 Everyday Lives Conference: Making it Happen
in Hershey, PA.. Since Barbara speaks from notes she
expanded on this topic for this book. She hopes to
present more on life in institutions in the future.

My parents put me in Menningerís because I wasn't welcome in
any school. In 1961, tax deductions were given for something
like Menningerís, but not for things like people coming in to
the home to give me attention or respite care. Mom and Dad
were on duty 24-7 and they were worn out. If someone had
been there to help Mom have time for herself, she would have
had the energy to deal with me. If someone could have given
me lots of one-on-one time and kept me busy, I could have

61

stayed out of a lot of trouble. If I had someone to take me to the park to run and play every day, I would have been a lot easier to live with. It also would have helped Mom if someone had helped with the housework. There would have been a lot less conflict and a lot less anxiety for both of us. Instead, I was placed in an institution. This was the most painful thing my parents ever went through. Giving a ten year old child away was unthinkable. Many, many tears were shed.

I had realized for several years that something was really wrong with me, but I was blamed for it. Even though I couldn't help my tics and frequent upsets, it was implied that I could "control them if I wanted to." I spent most of my life trying to tell people that things were often too intense for me, even when I was small. The people at Menninger's never got it. I am a lot less anxious in my present surroundings as an adult, where I have some control of my environment.

The psychiatrist I saw since I was five didn't help my Mom's attitude. I think he may have aggravated her feelings of guilt and shame. Whether or not that's true, Mom and I tossed guilt and shame back and forth like a hot potato for years.

When I arrived at Menninger's. I was 10. I was desperate for a cure. I had always overreacted to pain, but by the time I was 10, I was also reacting to loud noises the same way I did to getting hurt. I also often felt depressed. I was told that I enjoyed making myself miserable.

It took them three months to "find" me a therapist, even though they could have just assigned one who had time when I came. My arrival was not a surprise. They had two months or more to "look" for a therapist before I even walked in the door. Instead, they wasted three months of my life doing nothing.

The people at Menninger's had no explanation for what was wrong with me. They would keep asking me "why". All I could do is cry and say, "I don't know," and then rack my brains for the "reason." I could not convince anyone that I had sensory problems. People thought it was ìmentalî and talked as if I could just wish it away. Hopefully, autistic young people have it better than that now.

They were extremely preoccupied with my behaviour and would punish me for the smallest thing, with time-outs up to an hour long and taking away possessions which I was ìmisusingî or not letting me go somewhere. It is futile to try and change behaviour without changing the cause. I know how people should act, but I also know what itís like not to care because I am so overwhelmed. Then I get the silly idea that I have a right to misbehave because I feel so bad. The inner feelings control my behaviour. I want to be able to be in control on the inside so I can act right on the outside. But I can't always control my environment, which then leads to being overwhelmed on the inside and a loss of control of my behaviour.

They talked about "fantasy" as if it was an altered state of consciousnessóas being ìin fantasyî versus being "in reality." If I was too happy or excited about something (for them), they said I was "high" and that, too, was wrong. Behaviour was never regarded as obedient versus rebellious or good versus naughty. When they didn't like the way I acted, it was described as "sick." And then they would threaten that I would never go home until I "got well."

They never used words like reward and punishment at Menninger's, but who were they kidding? If I wasnít allowed to go somewhere because of my behaviour, what was it? In 1967 I had a funny thought of what it would be like if you put a comma between first and last names of people like you do places, as in "Topeka, Kansas." I laughed about it. I even told the worker why I was laughing. She didn't let me go to the carnival they were having at my school that day because I laughed. I hadn't done anything wrong except laugh at something that someone else didn't think was funny. And now they say that laughter is good for the immune system! ·

There was no occupational therapy at Menninger's to help people with sensory problems. All they did was the Freudian stuff - not the couch type, but the Freudian philosophy. All that talk about the subconscious mind. With that they could pin any idea or feeling on you that wasnít yours, such as calling church steeples phallic symbols. If that was true, why do female cathedrals have steeples? And why are steeples on or near the head, not the other end? I have never seen male privates anywhere symbolically. I have had thoughts about female parts. They are the only ones that I can relate to.

After a year I realized that I was no better, and I was sad. When I was almost 12, I had been at Menninger's for sixteen months. It had rained for days, and I was crying a lot. Thatís when the group Doctor said it would be at least five years before I'd "get well." Telling families that someone would get well in "years" bought them a lot of time to collect money and not help anyone get better. At that point I was put on Thorazine and Ritalin. I got much worse. I didn't know it was the drugs that made me sicker. No one was concerned about my sudden regression, as they should have been.

During the sixteen months I spent on neuroleptics and Ritalin, I avoided school and even my former favorite activities most of the time. I screamed a lot, and in the mornings I felt so bad that I didnít want to move or even talk, because it made me feel worse. I had always had OCD symptoms such as intrusive thoughts. They were much worse when I was on the drugs. That and severe anxiety made me feel hopeless, like I was dying before my time. I could see no future.

I was sure that the "best" hospital in the world was failing me. I knew that, just like my Mom, they'd just say, once I was destroyed, that I did it to myself. It grieves me the way the mental health people at the "best" hospital could make me sicker and then accuse me of NOT WANTING TO GET WELL. I cry out to God in my heart constantly to undo the damage done by their "help."

When I was 13, I was taken off the drugs and put in the older girls group. They got on to me more than ever before. No time outs but LOTS of scolding. I was told that "I didn't want to be helped" because I hated all this criticism. I hated the broken promises, the hope that they would help me "get well," and then, later, the realization of knowing that they didn't have a clue. They never said 'we don't have all the answers.' They just blamed me for "clinging to my illness."

What they called my illness was all the things I had to do to survive. They ignored the things that hurt me. They never asked, "What do you think would make you feel better or motivate you to try to do well?" Rewards for good behaviour were non-existent. No one ever said, "The teachers told us you did really well in class today, so you and I are going out for ice cream." Instead they focused on taking away privileges for supposed bad behaviour. I got the idea that, had I ever succeeded in stopping all that they disliked about me, they would have forgotten I was ever there. I would have become invisible.

I am very hungry for the warmth of real love based on unconditional acceptance. That's why I have had to personify objects. I could never be satisfied with people. Something BIG was always missing. I haven't found it yet. It's too easy for people to "treat" depression with a pill when the real need is for love and anything that will bring inner peace and happiness.

I had to beg, plead and manipulate for the simplest of privileges and activities that are common expectations for regular children. Then I was nagged about selfishness and pressured to think about others by these people who were pathologically independent and had NO NEED for anything I was able to share. Any time I showed an interest in anyone else, they accused me of being nosy. Wouldn't it have been better to use that interest to teach compassion? Everything was done for me by the staff. I could do nothing in return. I was trapped in an environment engineered to create ultra-dependency. The social atmosphere dictated "we don't need you" but never forget "you can't make it without us." This created a helplessness detrimental to any resemblance of mental "health." The staff was either unable or unwilling to recognize this.

I think we have to admit it: a mental hospital, even a good one where they had no restraints, no seclusion and used drugs sparingly (for most of my stay from 1961 to 1968 I was drug free), is an obedience school for children whom adults find annoying. There was no mental HEALTH there.

I was much more anxious and dysfunctional when I left Menningerís than before I had gone. I was older and supposedly "trained" but still very miserable. I never got any real help until I met a naturopath in 1980. It was only then that I had any hope for "getting well."

I hope that everyone who reads this can understand that I WAS NOT HELPED at all as far as my mental health was concerned. I did grow up and finish school, but I never did as well as I could have, thanks to the ìtreatmentî I received.

I think that there was a genius locked up inside me that had great promise. When I was ten, I was tested, and they told me that my IQ was so high that it couldn't be measured. I completed both 5th and 6th grades at age ten and entered 7th grade when I turned eleven. With the right kind of help I could have sailed through high school and college and made my parents very proud.

I did grow up and finish school, but I never did as well as I could have, thanks to the "treatment" with medication. I got Thorazine and couldn't function in school. I learned very little, and got a lot of D's in subjects that were formerly my favorites. Fortunately the drugs were stopped before I turned 13. Had I been on the drugs any longer, I am sure I would have had to stay in the institution for life. As it was, the drugs made me sick enough to be in constant pain throughout the rest of my school days. I never felt good in school again. Getting off the drugs made me able to stop trying to avoid school, but it never again was like it was before. Anxiety became a daily battle. Anxiety made it hard to learn, and I couldnít even consider taking certain subjects because they made my thinking go out of control.

I never learned a foreign language. Trying to process funny sounding words would set off nonsense syllables in my head and a sick feeling inside my body. I don't have a word to describe it - just painful. I also had a lot of problems with science and social studies because of the funny sounding words and names. I had loved geography before I went to the institution. After I was on Thorazine I went berserk because of the funny sounding place names in Latin America. When I was in a history class, I had intrusive thoughts about maps with people's names on them instead of place names. Without the drugs, a thought like that would have just made me laugh. With the drugs, the thoughts became intrusive and interfered with my being able to even stay in the classroom. American history should have been enjoyable, but I had so much anxiety that I learned no history at all. My formerly smart brain had crashed and burned.

I'll bet in time, with the right help and a decrease in my level of anxiety, I would have learned four years of Latin and then been able to learn other foreign languages. The DRUGS KILLED THAT! Because of the anxiety and the intrusive thoughts that came when I tried to do school work, I would have had severe panic anxiety attacks had I tried to learn a language. Learning languages should have been fun. I have always done well with English - why not Spanish, French or Norwegian. Then I could have gone to their countries and understood their language. I would have worked on a bigger vocabulary for places I would actually go to and found a friend to practice with. Even if I could find a cure for my original problem today, it would be hard to learn a lesson because of the association of pain with school.

Permanent changes in my body were caused by the drugs. I read that drugs cause problems in a short time. These changes can be seen on a really good MRI (one that can scan individual cells). This damage can be see in a matter of weeks. I took the drugs for 16 months. That was 125 mg. Thorazine daily for a little girl who only weighed 80 pounds and I think 20 mg. of Ritalin. For a while the neuroleptic was 5 mg. of Stelazine daily.

My parents wanted me to go on to college, but because of the after-effects of the drugs, I couldn't handle it. When I tried college, I often felt so anxious that it was almost like being back on the drugs again. I attended part-time for one year. At that point I regressed and developed compulsive behaviour that got me fired from my first job. I began screaming a lot again, too. No little girl should ever be given neuroleptics or any other drug because someone doesn't like the way they act. The advertisements lie. The child won't feel any better. And then, when the child feels worse, they are also blamed for that too.

Since I got so much sicker right in front of the teachers and the rest of the staff, it makes me wonder. Didn't they see that I was suddenly much worse than I'd ever been, after taking drugs for just two weeks? If this is what was "best" for me, I think I would have wanted something less than the best.

A friend in Wichita, who works with children with autism, says that she is sure that the long term effects of Thorazine, Stelazine and Ritalin from when I was eleven and twelve led to an increase in anxiety and noise sensitivity that I wouldn't have had if I had only had good nutrition and no drugs. She guessed that if my present condition and life as a teen had been drug free, that my autism alone would not have been so crippling. For example, on a scale of 1-10 with drugs: anxiety=10, noise sensitivity=10; without drugs: anxiety=3, noise sensitivity=7. In other words, noise would have still been a problem but maybe 30% less. Much of the "pain" that I feel from noise is a result of anxiety. Noise doesn't "hurt" my ears like it does some people's. With 70% less anxiety, noise would still be uncomfortable but it wouldn't make me want to scream. Without the drugs and with the possibility of being a college graduate, I could have had a good job and not ever needed social security for disability.

These days, people who choose to smoke are suing tobacco companies and winning. I wish I and/or someone else like me could sue the company which makes Thorazine and win millions of dollars. A lawsuit like that, repeated with about a dozen people, would certainly stop the forced drugging that I endured. Many people would be saved from a lifetime of mental illness.

Barbara Moran

In 3rd World Countries people who actually become psychotic usually get well. About 75% of them recover fully and live normal lives again and the rest improve and do better. This is without any drugs. These statistics are embarrassing to the mental health professionals in the United States. In our country, they don't get well. Most of them become chronic cases and live in board and care homes paid for by the state until they die.

Children love to learn, and they will unless it is ruined by the wrong kind of teaching environment. Autistic children don't need the confusing and loud environment. They do need to be around other children, though, and then do need a chance to go places and have an enriched environment. I think that children are on the bottom of the priority list. Just like the mental hospital, the school is there for the sake of the system.

In my opinion, sensory integration, floor time, social stories, a lot of one-on-one academic teaching and LOVE, along with good nutrition, can take the worst autistic person and make them college material. With the right kind of help, real help, someone like me could do really well in school and graduate from college with a Ph.D. and be financially independent. I truly hope that sharing my story gives others that chance. It is a privilege to be heard.

About the Author

Barbara Moran was born in South Dakota in 1951. Her family moved back to Omaha, Nebraska, in 1954 where her father, a pathologist, worked at St. Catherine's Hospital. Due to lack of support and understanding for the family, Barbara was placed in an institution at age ten, where she remained for seven years. She was then moved to a foster family where she lived for the next ten-and-a-half years. There was little emotional support in the foster family as they had no understanding or training in autism. They also had grandchildren during this time, who spent a lot of time in the home. The crying of the babies intensified Barbaraís noise sensitivity and anxiety level, which continues to this day. Barbara completed high school and took a full time job working in a nursing home, where she worked for 22 years.

Barbara currently lives in her own apartment in Topeka, Kansas, on social security disability. She is writing her autobiography and likes to draw traffic lights and cathedrals, the very things that Menningerís tried to cure her of in the sixties! Her artwork is on sale at autism conferences and ìoutsiderî art galleries.

Barbara was elected to the Board of Directors of the Autism National Committee in the fall of 2002 and is enjoying serving her term.

Barbara would like interested readers to contact her if you have questions, or are interested in a presentation.

Write to her at 2409 West 21 Street, Apt.6 Topeka, KS, 66604 or phone 785-235-8432.

Robert W. Cutler

When We Were Young

Presented at the Annual Conference of the Autism
National Committee, Atlanta, Georgia, 1997

I look forward to presenting in Atlanta to educate more people
about autism. FC has become my tool to talk about my life.
I can now change people's minds about who the real Robert
Cutler is. I am now ready to advocate for my good friends
across the world. Someday I will write a book to give parents
of children with autism hope. I am a living example. I survived
hell. Try topping that.

Medicine is not always an exact science. Any cure of
allergies? I want to be in control so I can help children who
have autism. My disability has taught my mother to become a
very vocal advocate. But I could help. My computer may not
be vocal, but the words I type will changes lives.

Teresa (sensory therapist) is a person with love in her
heart. Relaxed, restful time when I am with Teresa. She
clears my mind by touching my body. No one has made my mind

clearer with any drug. Bountiful energy when she is near. I just had to get that said.

I know now that I am born with an underdeveloped brain. I just have to give my brain a chance to index my thoughts. Just hunting for a cure with seizures, but autism has benefits. You never need to take notes because you remember everything.

About my family: I got opera young in Germany from my Da and Mom. I tried to be a good boy, but autism started to take control of my mind and soul. I now went down a path of destruction. For years I wandered through hell, seeking value. Da left us a long time ago because Robert was a bad boy. I miss Da because he did love Robert. I wish I could change the past, but I can't, so I live in pain because of what I did to my family. I am sorry that I ruined everyone's life. I only understood that I tried to be brave, but I panicked because I wanted to be a normal boy, instead of a useless piece of shit! Mom you tried to help me, but I failed you.

I needed to hear from you that it was not my fault. Mom, I know if you could, you would change things and decisions might have been different. But we need to continue the struggle. I could write a book about our trials and tribulations. I dream some day I will be respected for my intelligence and not my differences.

To my brother George: Robert wants to know why is it we are different, but so much alike, for example, we both like things in order. George you give me car rides, map reading, knowledge about sports. You, George, believe in yourself. I learned to believe in myself from typing words of Robert's mind on computers. You use the brains Mom helped you develop and you will be enriched. You typed [with Rob] today George. It works! Yes.

George, remember when we used to jump up and down on the beds? It would drive Mom crazy, but do you think that we can do it one more time? We are not too old. I was only joking, but it would be nice to go back like in the movie *Field of Dreams*. Movies help Robert communicate. I brought to Mom's house three baseball movies. I was able to say the words while eating breakfast, "I want to go to the Red Sox game."

George was a better father to me than Da. George, you are my brother and most of all my friend. Sherri is the sister I never had. I went to Colorado with Mom, George and Sherri (in 1981). I knew that George would marry her someday. Tell George to come to Disney World. I will not let him down. I want to spend some of my money I have because Steve from Fernald Penitentiary [state institution] did abuse me. Mom, I am not a wealthy man yet, but I want to show the people I love a good time. Five minutes in a room with Steve, George, Ross and Robert would have been nice, but Disney World is Justice. Who came to my rescue when I was suffering with panic attacks? Answer: Mark, Mom, George, too. I love you all for all your support and understanding. George, if something happens to Mom or Mark, promise to protect me from evil.

To an old friend: Ross should join the Circle [of Friends], so I can see more of him. I used to have fun with Ross when I was a boy. Love you, Ross. Welcome to my circle! Please join, Ross.

Grandpa and Grandma would be proud of all my successes. I planted flowers on Castle Island with Grandpa on September 6, 1968. I remember it like it was yesterday. I miss them both very much. I hope they see my typing from heaven!

I love all my cousins because they accept me for who I am and not my autism. But I love my Mom the most. I love cousin Rose because she tried to understand me. I miss Thanksgiving and Christmas parties. I am thinking about Grandpa and Gramma and have been playing *Pines of Rome.* I knew it drove her up the wall. But Grandma was a feisty woman sometimes, too. I wish Da's side accepted me. Too bad. I wish to be invited to their social events.

In my own home: Yesterday was Browing Road [group home]. Today is Lowell Street [apartment]. But tomorrow is my own house in Arlington, near Mom so you can walk over and ring my door bell.

Writing to Senator [Ted] Kennedy: On TV I heard they

want to cut education for people with disabilities. This is wrong because every human being in the world should be taught that all living things belong to God. We are here for a short time. John Kennedy's life was shortened by a bullet, but we still talk about his ideas. I will tell this to Ted [Senator Kennedy]. Also, I will ask him to see his sister Rosemary and bring her back to Hyannis to live in her home. Time to heal the past mistakes. There is nothing better than the smell of the ocean and being able to walk on the shoreline with a friend or sister or brother. I walk in Maine or on Castle Island. Maybe I can walk with you with, Rosemary, in Hyannis someday.

**Information about the author and how
to contact him follows the next essay,
which is also by Rob Cutler**

Pull the Plug on Aversive Treatment

The following presentation was made at the
March 20, 2002, meeting of the
New Hampshire Task Force on Autism.

I am here to ask you to pull the plug on aversive treatment. Why is behaviorism, pain, and aversive treat-ment running wild in autism treatment? Why is shame and pain used? What ever happened to human rights for all? I am a man recovering from the ruins of behavioral force. Behaviorism was used to destroy my will, but I hung onto my sanity.

Should a person with a disability be allowed to stop their treatment without parental consent if they feel the pain is too much? Yes!

How much physical and mental damage was done to people with disabilities who were used as lab rats so behaviorists could ply their trade of "curing" us? Applied behavior analysis (ABA) is like a snake medicine. If you want us to imitate and not think or function, then use ABA. But if you want us to function in society and fully participate, then use facilitated communication (FC), occupational therapy, sensory integration and good doctors. The choice is easy. FC is the way. ABA will run rampant in the world. It will become aspiring for all kinds of behavior issues. But the cold, harsh reality is that ABA in its purest sense is Nazism. Choices are zero under this regime. They control a group of inferior people and dumb them down further. FC, on the other hand, lifts our voices and gives us hope for a new tomorrow instead of reliving yesterday's controlling past. We need to show parents and teachers that there are better ways, yes!

Behavior modification is guesswork. People with autism need challenges, not boring workshops. Restraint is not an answer, period! Study autism before you use the behavioral stuff on us and instead use the power to empower my friends who use FC as their voice.

Behaviorism is a compliance control model based on coercion. Coercion is not really education. The behavioral technician at best uses rewards or withholds them to force the student into compliance. This ignores the needs of the individual who may need more time, space or quiet. At worst, painful punishments or deprivations are inflicted. Many of the goals may be trivial or inappropriate, for example, timing out a toddler for crying.

ABA does not require an understanding of the disability, in this case, autism. Many ABA techniques ignore the basic needs of the individual with autism. For example, the so-called firm "NO" violates the auditory sensitivity of the individual with autism.

ABA is starting to give merely lip service to the sensory and environmental issues only if such considerations do not interfere with the collections of data. The concern with data overrides appropriate responses to the child who may be overwhelmed by sensory and environmental issues. If the technicians were to respond in the right way, i.e., support the child, it would mess up the data and the data is rules all.

True choice is absent in ABA. The technician picks the rewards and controls them while also picking the tasks and goals.

ABA acts like it created structure and task analysis. These existed even before Betty Crocker was making cakes and the ancient Romans were building aqueducts for Rome's plumbing.

Structure and predictability are important. Keeping the student informed about what is going on is merely respectful. Task analysis for motor tasks (this of course requires an understanding of the motor aspects of autism which is often lacking) can be helpful. But hundreds of repetitions for the sake of compliance can be foolish, cruel or disrespectful.

Over-training in speech and movement for people with autism who have motor planning issues can make our people with autism appear foolish and inappropriate. An example is forcing complete sentences when most typical people would use a phrase or a gesture, such as requiring "I want the milk in the red cup, please," when one might say, "More milk, please," or even just hold up the cup. Let the differences be honest in autism rather than behaviorally forced.

Many behaviorists try to frighten parents into using ABA because they tell them their children will end up in institutions. These fear tactics are unconscionable. Also unconscionable are the assumptions made about people with autism—that we are noncompliant, antisocial, uncaring are simply not true. Such false assumptions are used to bolster the rigid and sometimes cruel practices of Lovaas and ABA.

Let's not forget about those children who are so traumatized by ABA that they cry when the doorbell rings, refuse to go into the room where they are "trained" (not taught), have bad dreams which may persist as Post Traumatic Stress Disorder after the behavioral technicians leave.

Parents, I know your child loves you in spite of the critics.

About the Author

Robert W.P. Cutler, Jr. is a strong self-advocate with autism who wants to communicate his understanding and experiences in autism and his views on the delivery of services and the rights of persons to communicate and to use facilitated communication. His story "Not To Yield" has been published in Hank Bersani's *Responding to the Challenge: Essays in Honor of Gunnar Dybwad* and in the OPILCOP Brief in the Olmstead case heard before the U.S. Supreme Court.

Mr. Cutler is Immediate Past President of the Autism National Committee and a member of the Board of the Herb Lovett Memorial Foundation. He has presented at conferences including TASH, Northeast Regional Conference on Autism, Rosemary Dybwad Memorial Lecture, Herb Lovett Taking the Leap Conference, Massachusetts Department of Mental Retardation, Pennsylvania Office of Mental Retardation, Syracuse Facilitated Communication Institute, National Institute of Health Working Group on Autism, University of Massachusetts Medical School, University of New Hampshire Institute on Disability and the Autism National Committee in California, Connecticut, Georgia, Massachusetts, Maine, Pennsylvania, New York, Maryland, Michigan, New Hampshire, Washington, D.C., and in England.

He writes a column—"Ask Rob"—for the *Communicator*, newsletter of the Autism National Committee. He was appointed to the State Advisory Council for Massachusetts Department of Mental Retardation by the Governor and also serves on the New Hampshire Task Force on Autism.

Mr. Cutler lives in Arlington in his own home supported by staff and very near his family. He is challenged not only by autism and a severe movement disorder but by post-traumatic stress and seizure disorders as well.

Robert was mis-diagnosed and put away in the Fernald Penitentiary (state school) when he was 24. There he was treated like and felt like a criminal: punished, starved, restrained, beaten and locked in a dark room, not because he was bad, but because no one understood autism, allergies and the sadness in his heart. A sadistic staff member, who was later convicted for this abuse, tortured him at night with beatings. Since this was pre facilitated communication, Rob had no way to communicate what was happening to him. He remained in Fernald until he was 29 years old. He is trying to put this pain behind him; to forget it, but the flashbacks continue.

In spite of these difficulties, Mr. Cutler is a strong and active advocate. He believes in the universal right of all to be included in the community and vigorously opposes all attempts to institutionalize, restrain and use other extreme coercive means against people with disabilities.

Contact Robert at robcutler@aol.com

David Goodman

Things That Bother Me

Presented at the Autism National Committee
Conference, 1999.

Editors note: *David is a man who is able to speak and to type. Like many on the spectrum, his ability to type is stronger than his ability to clearly vocalize his thoughts. This presentation demonstrates both types of communication. The initial part (short phrases) is what was spoken. The second portion (in paragraph form) was his response to a question about the speech on his keyboard.*

People talking to another person and not responding to me
The noise from the vacuum cleaner
Kids and babies crying and screaming in public
Construction work
Doorbell
Songs I don't like on the radio
A horn that sounds different in a car
Fire truck, tornado warnings
People coughing and snoring at night.

What helps me relax:
Good music that I like
Going to the movies, to lunch.
Helping mom grocery shop
Taking breaks at work
Taking walks around
Bowling
Activities with my group

I would like people to know that I have trouble understanding. People can support me by paying attention to me. Yes, people not understanding very well, with what's going on with everything and having trouble talking and hearing everything that's going on. It's like the voices that are too loud. People need to talk softly. One voice at a time works out okay for me. It's like not hearing and understanding everything. It's easier to talk when they're fun sports for me to go and see once in a while. There are crowds on the subway and they make me feel nervous but I do well.

I feel very happy about being on the board and I would like the board to help me out some more by giving me some support like better support like giving me more time to answer and speak softly. I would like to help the board out some more. I would to help the board understand more about autism.

I want people to understand that I have trouble thinking of ideas about what to do on the weekends when I run out of plans.

David Goodman

My friends are very important because they like me. Some of my coworkers are hard and some are easy. Some put too much pressure on me by giving me too much to do. I just cope with it. Dina puts too much pressure on me on the phone.

I feel happy about moving into my own apartment with Bruce.

About the Author

David Goodman is 32 years old and lives in a condominium in Rockville, Maryland. He graduated from Sherwood High School in Olney, Maryland and has worked as an office automation clerk for the National Institutes of Health since 1991. He is a member of the board of directors of the Autism National Committee. He enjoys bowling, watching sports on TV, going to the movies and getting together with friends.

Contact David at SusanG1961@aol.com

Stephen Hinkle

Growing up with Autism: The Value of Inclusion and Disability Awareness in School

Early Years of My Life

When I was very little, I just thought I was another little Boy. Then, when I was diagnosed with autism, I just thought that something was different but did not know what about me was different. Something about me was very different than normal people my age.

My mom had me be in many medical studies. I could never figure out why I was in so many medical studies. My mom did not tell me what any of them were about. I probably could not understand much at that age. Actually, I learned later that they were autism research—research about my immune system. These medical studies were long and involved lots of psychological tests and blood tests which I hated.

I did not have many friends, but I did not know why. At that time, I had no idea what I was missing out on. I did not know how to make friends or the social aspects.

For some of the time, when I was real young, I slept in 20-minute stretches. I never slept through the night until I was about three years old. This made it very hard for my mom to care for me. I sometimes kept her up during the night.

In addition, I had food allergies. One of them was milk and another was corn syrup. The doctors did not diagnose this correctly, so my mom pulled me off a lot of things, and I was on rotation diets until I was finished with elementary school.

I went to preschool at a Montessori school. Preschool was fun, although some kids made fun of me. I loved all the activities of preschool. I learned to play games, count, to read little kid books, and the like.

Elementary School

When I seven years old, I was diagnosed with autism. A psychiatrist said to my dad, "Good thing you make a great living because he has to go into an institution real soon." My mom ignored him, and I eventually progressed much farther than the physiatrist would have ever imagined! As a matter of fact, if my mom had done what he said, I would not be writing this today.

My dad was a TV news director, so we moved a lot. I went to several elementary schools. I started in segregated classes for grades K-4. I was not challenged; most of the work was remedial or completely different from the normal curriculum. I did not know why I was excluded from many special activities, including field trips. For one field trip, my mom actually threatened to have the American Civil Liberties Union sue the district if they did not let me go. Because of this, they finally did let me go.

I also had bad handwriting. People said to my mom that I

would not succeed if I had bad handwriting. To justify getting me a computer, she showed them her doctors' handwriting, her lawyer's handwriting, and the handwriting of some other people with high paying jobs. This justified the school system purchasing me a computer to use at school. I had a desktop placed in my classroom in grade 5, and a laptop for grade 6 and on.

In the fourth grade, they mainstreamed me into one class, Science. I began to know what a real class is like, because I learned two sets of rules. My mom asked me, "Why do you behave differently there?" and I replied, "Because the rules are different there." Learning two sets of rules is a bad example for anyone when one of them is incorrect for the same environment.

In the fifth grade, I was fully included for the first time. However, I used the resource room some, and I continued to receive speech therapy. This was the first time I got to experience many things about being a normal student, but I still needed help with homework and still had few friends. This was a big jump for me. Because of the segregated classes, I was behind academically, so many skills most kids learn in grades 2-4, I did not learn. I had some fun experiences, though. "Fun Runs" and "Oceanography Field Day" were some of the highlights of the year. These I did look forward to.

We moved again before 6th grade. Sixth grade was the worst year of my entire student career. I had mean teachers. I sometimes followed the janitors around all day. They had me in remedial classes. The only plus was that this is the first time I could use a laptop computer to take notes and write on in class. The only good thing that came out of this was that I knew "good" from "bad" in terms of teaching.

Middle School (7-8)

We moved before 7th grade. In 7th grade, I was happier. Many of the teachers wanted things to work for me. I enjoyed many things like getting to take more advanced computer classes, industrial arts, etc. I still had no friends or social life. I did have one mean teacher in 8th grade. Middle School was a good success for me. The curriculum was interesting, and the school had a "family theme", now known as a "school within a school" concept. I had some accommodations (for example, speech therapy, test accommodations). One problem was running out of time on standardized tests; another was that the word processor they bought me would not type the math symbols I needed. When this need arrived, they took care of it.

High School (9-12)

I was included in many classes. I got to take some classes I really love, like programming. I did some work independently, because I had trouble with the material, particularly in literature and social studies. I even ended up taking some advanced classes, such as calculus, AP physics, AP computer science, and the like.

One of the fun parts of high school is that I got to be involved in technical crew for many stage shows, including *Oklahoma*, *The Nutcracker*, *Little Shop of Horrors*, and others. This was one of the few extracurricular activities I was involved in. I also did tech crew for a local dance company that rented the school theater.

It took me one extra year to finish, but two very special people wanted me to have it be a special one. I did not have many friends and get to participate in much until the senior year. Claire Roush, a teacher's aide, and Anne Callies, the speech pathologist decided to give me social skills training. She helped me learn some basic social skills such as interacting and the like. She also arranged for me to go to the senior activities. One of their first "homework" assignments was to go to the homecoming dance. Then they had me go to other activities, like a football game, a basketball game, prom, senior breakfast, Graduation, and Grad Nite. I also managed to graduate with above a 3.0 GPA, which allowed me to enter San Diego State University.

College

I applied to SDSU just like a normal person would. I got accepted, and I never took the SAT Test! College has been a challenge for me. I have been doing okay, though. I have had some bad teachers, and had to retake a class, but I did okay. I am a computer science major. The good part is that I learned a lot of new stuff. For example, in CS440 I learned many useful things about computer ethics. I also did a special study in web page design to learn HTML, JavaScript, and the like.

I am now even taking some classes for a degree that have been really hard for me. I have taken English, Writing, Anthropology, Religion, and some others. I had to get tutoring for them. I learned something about myself. I am bad at inferring what the author of a text does *not* tell you. This has been hard, especially with relationship ethics, which has always been my weak point, because I have never dated nor had a boyfriend/girlfriend or close friend relationship.

The college is good on accommodations. First of all, they have a whole department that deals with accommodating people with disabilities. They can provide many types of accommodations and even some modifications to the curriculum (not required by the law). All professors are required to honor what the DSS office says, or DSS will come after them.

I am now pressured to get a degree. Originally I planned just to take classes and get a job. Some of the basic requirements are boring, but with accommodations I can make it through.

This has led me to a job at City Heights Educational Pilot where I work as a network tech and web grade book programmer. I do a lot of computer related stuff. I also work hard to fix computers. Another task is to build the web code for the grade books for distance learning courses offered by the Interwork Institute project.

I have found some people to continue teaching me social skills, Deborah and Ron Plotkin. Oddly, I met Deborah in the tech booth when I was in high school, on a *Nutcracker* show for Super Kids Dance Studio. I never knew she did this until years later. Regional Center said they had no one to teach these skills, yet Deborah was vendorized with the regional center, which explains how much the system tries to get out of paying. Now, I work with Deborah on social skills at the college level. Our plans include learning how to make friends. I hope to have a social life soon. Deborah is teaching me how to meet people, how to ask someone to do things, how to carry on conversations, how to interact and have a meal with someone else, and the like. Eventually, she wants me to go to clubs, activities, and lots of fun stuff! She also helps me with my educational curriculum and housekeeping skills.

I am now working out, trying to lose some weight. I attend the fitness center regularly, and I am eating a bit less. I enjoy working out and running on the treadmill and elliptical.

My Recommendations for Others with Disabilities in an Inclusive Setting

I am going to give some advice to all parents and to students with disabilities to help stand up for their rights to be able to make it through the system. This can be a difficult and trying process.

Elementary School

Elementary school is the beginning of a new world for children! This can be a fun and exciting world for them. However, when I was in elementary school, I did not know what school was about. Many people are excited to start elementary school. Many things are new to them, like getting on the school bus for the very first time, having teachers, being in class, knowing the rules of the classroom, as well as knowing what the subjects are like math, reading, writing, history, science. There are often fun specials like library, PE, art, and music.

People with disabilities may have trouble with this transition. They go from a world of being at home to a world of having to be at school in the morning to mid-afternoon. Why this is happening may be a mystery to them.

When I was in elementary school, I was in segregation

until grade 4. I did not know why I was only mainstreamed for specials like PE and art. Some of my teachers were mean. I also was cheated out of things other people were taught like time management and note taking skills. I was good in math, though.

Students have their strengths and weaknesses for different subjects. For me, my strength was math and science, but my deficit was handwriting. People with disabilities' profiles may look more like a bunch of ups and downs than a straight line, but we all have strengths and weaknesses, don't we? Even if the student is weak in an area, do not stop them from expanding on their strengths, because that will often lead them to a career down the road.

Homework is another issue. Students wonder why they are sent home with a lot more work to do. You may have to explain this one. Sometimes, people with disabilities do not know where to get help with homework, or forget to carry books back and forth to school. For this, I suggest a "two sets of books accommodation." I also suggest tutoring, if they need it.

Elementary school is important because it gives students the building blocks of everyday life—reading, writing, spelling, grammar, math, as well as introductions to science, computers, and history, which are used almost every day. Most elementary schools have a "special" class period rotation system that give the students in their first years fun things to explore like art, music, PE, and computer lab.

The curriculum for people with disabilities should be taught step by step, to make it clear to them how to do things, and how to get help if they need it. By breaking into steps, this teaches how a big assignment can be managed and not overwhelm the young student.

If the student with a disability communicates a different way, or has an aide or paraprofessional with them, make sure the other students know why the aide is there, and that the other students interact with the person with a disability. If the other students understand what disabilities are at this level, they will treat them as part of their environment and accept them in school and in the general society the rest of their lives.

Behavior is another important step. It is important for people to learn class behavior early as it will impact them down the road. I learned better behaviors in an inclusive environment than in a segregated class. In the segregated class, there are no good role models. When I was mainstreamed into science in grade 4, my mom asked my why I behave differently there. I said because the rules are different there. This is an example of knowing the difference between segregation and inclusion.

I also recommend inclusion as a benefit for the other students, to make the class more interesting by having someone with a disability in the class. If a student with a disability is too disruptive, there are creative ways that can be used, including behavior analysis, assistive technology, or differentiating the instruction. For example, I heard that someone who had trouble with talking out and being disruptive was included in a regular class and used a *Touch Light* to call the teacher. This prevented the student, who could not raise his hand, from talking out. The teacher asked "Can I get a touch light for every student?" She got one for each student, and she had one of the quietest classes ever in her teaching career!

If students have poor handwriting, get them a computer to use! Doctors, lawyers, CEOs of companies, and other high-ranking people often have bad handwriting, and it does not impact their jobs.

Involve them in the special classes that are offered at an elementary school such as art, music, PE, library, and computer lab. These allow kids to express their talents in a variety of areas and be creative. Studies show that students who have taken courses in the arts do better overall academically.

Another accommodation I recommend is teaching the kids social skills and implementing "extracurricular inclusion." They may have deficits in this area, and these deficits will haunt them the longer this is not addressed. Learning social skills will allow them to have friends and have a life. They will have a good reason to want to stay at school if they get to attend the talent shows, carnivals, open houses, dance nights, assemblies, lunchtime recess, field day, and many other activities that elementary schools offer.

Explain the real uses of the knowledge they learn if they ask. Sometimes I asked, "When will we use this and for what?" This helps them know there is a benefit to learning the subject matter, and that it is not wasted time for them.

If they are doing poorly, or do not want to do something, ask why. If they are having trouble with something, it is a sign that they may need some accommodations, curriculum modifications, or assistive technology. For example, I needed extra time on tests. I did not want to take tests because I kept running out of time or was afraid to do poorly. In addition, their feedback can also be used to set IEP goals, or identify other issues.

Transition to Middle School or Junior High

Think back when you left 5th or 6th grade and you were going to now attend middle school or junior high school. You were at the age where you liked to be on a little adventure, and I bet you thought you knew everything in the world. I bet you had a lot of friends and wondered "what's next"?

Middle School (or Junior High) can be a big change for a student from elementary school. Students go from a world of a small campus to a medium size campus, a world of work and play to a world of work only. The course load is usually more. They go from having one classroom, where the teacher watches out for them all day, to a world where they have different teachers for different subjects and have to change classrooms every 40 to 100 minutes, depending on the schedule of the school. At some schools there may be lockers to store books. Many schools have no recess break, either.

The first thing I suggest is to give them time to adjust to changing classes. Whether your school offers standard, block, rotation, or another time schedule system, it can take some time getting used to for the student. One of the hard parts for me was going to the bathroom and getting to class in the five minute passing time allocated for changing classes.

Most of the academic classes at this level expect that students can take notes almost as fast as the teacher talks. I had some trouble with this. One accommodation I used for this is taping lectures. Another was the use of a laptop, word processor or computer. Also, the teachers expect students to have mastered a lot of skills taught in elementary school.

Another thing that is new is that most PE classes require changing and showering. This can take a while to get used to because of the short time constraints and all the extra work you must do before you come on or off the field or weight room.

There are many facilities at this level, like gyms, auditoriums, and specialized science labs, which most elementary schools do not have. This may seem strange. Explain the correct behaviors and features of the new facilities to the student, as this will help them know what to do when they are there.

A middle school class may require significantly more workload than an elementary school class. This can get people with disabilities overwhelmed by having to do more work than they can handle. Explain the steps and take things one step at a time. That way, they learn to do what overwhelms them at the beginning.

A typical middle school or junior high curriculum includes several subjects. Often they include language arts (or English), math, science, history, PE, computers, and a special period or elective period, which is often a student's choice. Elective classes can include foreign languages, music, art, drama, technology, wood shop, consumer and family studies, and several other choices which can vary from school to school

Middle school curriculum is getting tougher every day. For example, algebra is now a required eighth grade course, and English proficiency is a big concern. People may be put into remedial classes when they get to high school if they are not proficient enough in reading, causing them to lose electives (which is no fun for any student).

In evaluating reading, with all the standardized testing, it is important to test with both narrative and factual (non-fiction) technical reading. Many people with disabilities have trouble with inferring. In addition, some people read non-fiction better than fiction or vice versa. Most reading tests have been fiction-biased. By testing with both, you do not remediate someone who is actually capable just because of a low test score.

Have the student learn to interact in groups. That way they get to know some of the other classmates. This also teaches them to work with others and gives other students a chance to interact with someone with a disability. This helps them have someone to turn to, if they have a problem. Group work is a big part of middle school.

If they have trouble with assignments, ask them why. If they refuse to explain, there is often something wrong. Explain to them where and how to get help. Sometimes, keeping up the pace is the hardest thing if they are getting stumped somewhere. In fact, knowing the "chain of command" is a good idea as well.

If your school offers picking some classes the student wants, let the student with a disability choose something they are interested in. If you say they can't, and they really want to try, you are underestimating them! I believe that anyone can reach his or her goals and dreams.

If they get ahead in one area but behind in another subject, let them excel in the one they are good at. Often, this will lead them to a successful career in the future.

Get the accommodations you need. People with disabilities can get accommodations in regular classes. The students may need test accommodations, speech therapy, and other accommodations. Get them immediately. If you wait, the student suffers (which happened to me).

Curriculum modifications can help if the student is struggling. If the state mandates something, if necessary go to the minimum amount that they mandate for academic credit. I oppose classes that do not count for anything. For example, if the state standards mandate the student do two reports for credit in history, and the class does four, the person with a disability can just do two and still get credit.

A presentation to the class of why a student with a disability is different also helps the other students know about disabilities and that the behaviors the student with a disability does are not weird. I believe that teaching disability awareness in the curriculum is important. Lori Mitchell mentioned that learning that everyone is unique and that we are all "just like each other" is important.

Middle schools often have many types of clubs and activities, including dances, dress up days, plays, concerts, clubs, but students with disabilities may not even know where to go, much less how to get involved. Teach them this and have them pick some clubs they are interested in. This will help them make friends and enjoy the fun side of school. They may not know what they are missing if they have never been there. Extracurricular inclusion is necessary for "full inclusion"!

Transition to High School

In this transition, the workload is harder, and there is pressure to get good grades and to score high on the SAT test to get into college. People at that age are often into boyfriends and girlfriends. There is also a big emphasis on sports teams that compete against other schools. The social aspect is important at this age. Decisions made in high school will have impact on early adult life.

It is different from middle school, where kids think they know everything there is to know about everything. In high school, kids feel all grown up and think that they are adults already. The atmosphere feels different - every thing is bigger, classes are more pressured, and there is more homework. The campus size is larger, and getting around takes more time to get used to.

High School Classes

High school classes involve a lot of essays, and other kinds of writing. This can be frustrating, unless someone knows the format correctly. This is important to be taught. It is imperative that students have good writing skills for their reports. Learning to research things from the library is an important skill to master. Knowing how to use books, magazines, encyclopedias, the internet, and the like effectively is important to teach! Citing sources is also a good skill.

Math classes can be fast paced and get hard with so many problems to do. Reducing the workload a little can help, but do not go below the level that would cause the class to not give credit. The California state standards are getting strict here with geometry, Algebra 2, and trigonometry being requirements. Many high school kids take calculus or discrete math in their senior year.

If a student takes too long to get homework done, not letting them have time for other things, complain to the teacher. There may be ways to help. Get tutoring if necessary. The amount of homework that people with disabilities have should be reasonable, not overwhelming. However, do not leave out any skill because it is important if the student wants to go on to college.

Explain to students how to get help. This is important. This is an age where they may need to know the chain of command. If they have a problem, they need to act on it immediately, because otherwise they will get behind.

At the IEP meeting, explain to the teachers the accommodations the student will use in class for all subjects, such as testing time, use of a computer, paraprofessional, etc. Make sure they are comfortable with this. If not, see if there is another teacher that teaches the same class, or have them go to a conference on inclusion.

The student needs a 3.0 GPA or higher if his goal is to go to college. Many colleges have the same admission requirements whether the students have a disability or not. This is especially important, if the goal is to go directly from high school to a four-year college. If the goal is to go to a two-year community college, this is not as big a problem, but taking special education "not for credit" classes can cause some people to have to take remedial classes at college.

Let the student pick the classes if choices are offered. Many high schools require some combination of English, math, science, computers, history, fine arts, performing arts, practical arts, foreign language, and PE to graduate. Given this, many schools give choices in the course work for many subject areas. Let the student pick the best choice after discussing the workload and their interests.

For the major academics, choose what is recommended for college admission. If the student is advanced in an area, and most people have some strengths, go for advanced, AP, or other challenging courses in those subject areas.

I suggest not overloading the student. If it takes more than four years to graduate, that is okay. It took me five. However, it is not a good idea to do meaningless, functional skills type courses in segregation. This is the old approach which seriously limits the job potential of the student and cuts off the ability to attend college. If someone does not have the right classes to graduate or to get into college, it can seriously impact their adult life.

Get any test accommodations they need put into their IEP. That way, accommodations will apply to national tests. Many standardized test companies such as ETS (makers of SAT, ACT, and AP tests) will allow the IEP test accommodations to be used on their exams.

Also, educate the teachers about the various accommodations. It is important that the student be involved in how this is going. If they are having trouble, act on it now.

In California, and other states as well, there may be a required exam to graduate from high school. The impact for kids in special education is negative. Right now, there are lawsuits pending in some states which will probably allow accommodations and modifications to be used on these exams or provide an alternate test in some cases.

Teach them about all the clubs and activities and how to get involved. Explain what different activities are and help get them involved in something they are interested in, to get the full social benefit of school. It was not until grade 12 that I learned some social skills and what I was missing all these years. When they are finished with high school, they should participate in the celebration activities like Prom, Senior Breakfast, Yearbook Signing, Graduation, and Grad Nite (activities may vary by school).

If your district has a "funding cut-off" policy that prevents access to transition services if a student graduates with a real diploma, change it NOW. This policy encourages people to stay in high school until 22 and not graduate. This is not a good model, with many jobs requiring college, and many colleges requiring high school diplomas for admission. It causes many people with disabilities to be behind in their age interests when they enter college or vocational school.

Plan for after high school in the mid-high school years. Where does the student want to be in 5 years? In 10 years? Does the student wish to attend college or other post secondary education?   What field or type of job does the student want to have in the workforce? What type of education is needed (high school, college, graduate school, vocational training, entering an academy, etc.)? Does the student want to live on his own someday? Get married and have a family? What else is important to them in society?

High School Diplomas are needed for most jobs in the workplace these days and to be admitted to most universities. I feel sad how many people with disabilities are held until 22 and do not graduate, and are therefore limited to minimum wage jobs.

Employment and Internships

I find it sad that many people with disabilities end up at Burger King and McDonalds and other meaningless, low-paying, no-future kinds of job, when in reality they could have much better jobs. Often the system just finds them any job, when they should be looking in fields and sectors the person is interested in. For example, if someone selected technology as their field, they should look for jobs in computer, Internet, and specialized high-tech jobs. If the person selected arts, look for jobs at music companies, theaters, dance studios, film studios, art museums, and similar entities. If someone wants retail as their field, they should look at various stores that deal in retail goods.

People with disabilities should not be limited to poverty class jobs only. I would love to see some people with disabilities end up with middle class or wealthy class salaries with full benefits.

Job Coaches can be used to help people train and learn the work habits and ethics. The relationship should be productive and comfortable for the worker. The student in transition should be involved in the job coach selection and have recourse if the relationship does not work out for them.

Adult Life

One of the important factors of life after high school is to have a social life. This includes things like going to the movies, the theater, ballgames, museums, out to eat, bowling, and many other fun activities. After all, what would life be without them? Sadly, I see many people with disabilities end up not having friends.

Another common adult goal is to have a family of your own. I know several people with disabilities who are married. Some I know are even raising their own children.

Aides, Paraprofessionals, Job Coaches, Supported Living Workers, and the Like

The relationship between a student and his/her assistants or aides needs to be productive and comfortable for the student. Aides should allow an amount of error tolerance before they intervene or correct, which allows the student to be a normal person of their age and not be "glued" to each other. Error tolerance is the practice of allowing the student to mess up and get something wrong, and even fall flat on their face once in a while!   This may seem wrong when they have someone helping them, but how would they learn anything if they were never allowed to fail at some point?   They can't!!!!

Additionally, the student should be allowed some time to himself or herself. The student should be allowed to give feedback to their workers. Ultimately, they should have the right to fire them, if they are too upset or not getting along, or they are not getting any benefits from them being around.

These workers should help in a positive way and not hinder the student's progress or the student becoming too dependent on them. Ultimately, service workers should be more like an aide for everyone in the class or at work. They should be there for the student that needs them, but not be stuck to them.

Feedback

Student feedback is critical to accomplishing goals and in the IEP and ITP process. The student is the only one who has first hand experience with the quality of education they get, and how the curriculum, goals, accommodations, and modifications are working in the classroom.   Teachers have their side, but sometimes the conclusions the teacher reaches can be incorrect because of a problem they are not aware of.

For example, I had to do a test that required me to memorize all the data about some articles. I cannot memorize very well, and so I failed. I explained this, but they did not listen to me.

Regular feedback and investigation of complaints from the student are CRITICAL to the student's success. These should be included in the student's goals. The student should be at his/her planning meetings such as IEP and ITP or even run the meeting (for 4th grade and up). The parents can only offer a portion of this feedback, because they have not experienced first hand what happens, nor are they in class all day.

Even, if the child is not old enough to attend an IEP meeting, I suggest asking them, "Are you comfortable in the environment you are in?" "What are you doing well?" "What are you having trouble in?" "If you could change something, what would it be?" "What suggestions do you have?" "What should I tell your parents and teachers about how you are doing?" and others. These can go a long way to getting a good IEP and accomplishing goals.

Setting Goals of Their Very Own

There should be goals in the student's plans that are set by the student. It is okay if parents or teachers set some goals, but at least one goal at minimum should come from the student. This is important because it is their life and their education, and they should be able to get what they want and enjoy out of it.

This is also important because the parents will then know what their child wants to do with his life. These student-set goals do not have to be complex, but may be simple, like "I want to learn this," or "I want to get an A in this," or "I want be in the school play," "I want to make the basketball team," "I want to buy my own lunch," etc. It gives the student a sense of getting somewhere.

Conclusion

I want to conclude by telling you that it is all about students and making them succeed in life. That is what the school system should devote its resources to. Every student of all ages, all sizes, all with different strengths and weaknesses can learn together and accomplish their goals and reach their dreams!

Stephen Hinkle

About the Author

Stephen Hinkle is a 25 year old student who is currently attending San Diego State Univeristy. He is working towards a degree in computer science. He also works as a computer technician for the San Diego State Foundation. Stephen is an active advocate promoting human rights for everyone with disabilities. He presents whenever he can, usually focusing on inclusion in education and in the community. In his spare time, Stephen combines his love of music and his technical ability to promote the sharing of information. He also volunteers at this high school and the local children's services center, happy to share his expertise on the computer with those who need it.

You can contact Stephen with comments and questions at stphinkle@aol.com

Maegan Stoddard Gracia

An Inner Voice Set Free

Presented at the FC Conference, Autism Society of
America, Massachusetts Chapter, 1999

I am Maegan Stoddard Gracia, and I am autistic. I am very
pleased to be here with you today to share my experiences
with autism and facilitated communication (FC) with all of you.
It is good to know there are still people out there who are
interested in FC and how it affects our plight in life. Being
autistic and trying to have an existence as normal as possible
is an extremely difficult endeavor to undertake. With the
advent of FC, it has become somewhat easier.

To say that FC has changed my life would indeed be an
understatement. Imagine being in a world where you cannot
communicate at all your thoughts and feelings. A world where,
if you are sick, you cannot let anyone know, nor when you hurt,

emotionally or physically. In order to compensate for this, you create these horrendous behaviors to act out every emotion you cannot express, even happiness. This is all your body knows how to do, the only function it will perform for you. You know inside of your head and heart what you would want to say and do, but the dreadful autism will not allow these thoughts and actions to come through. This was my life for thirteen years! Then, like a miracle, FC came into my life and I had a voice! I could speak whenever I wanted and say anything I wanted. God was surely smiling down on me at that time, making sure the school I was attending (a segregated school for the disabled) decided to try FC out on some of their students. I was one of the students they felt could benefit from FC. I cannot fully express how wonderful life seemed to me when I first started to FC. Just to be able to tell my mother how I was feeling, things that bothered me, and to tell my family and friends how much I love them was a glorious feeling far beyond anything I had ever imagined happening to me. My entire life changed, people realized that I was a very intelligent person, and a very opinionated one at that. We could now think of me going into regular classes and getting the kind of education I was not only entitled to, but deserved to get. People, who used to stare at me as if I were doing nothing but taking up space, suddenly realized that I was a person to contend with. I had very strong feelings about life, God and people, and I soon let them know where I stood. I never hesitated to give my opinion when asked for it.

A new stage in my life started, an age of intelligence. I started taking honors classes at my neighborhood school, and excelled at them, to the amazement of a lot of people. The Standard Times, our city newspaper, even did an article about me and the progress in my life with FC. I made friends and had a very normal junior high experience.

I would love to tell you that everything was a bed of roses from then on, but we all know when dealing with autism and FC, this is never true. There are always mountains to climb and obstacles to overcome. In my case, the teacher who had been working with me left that position for another one, and I was sacrificially thrown to the lambs. The school department did not do such a good job finding a replacement.

My high school years were filled with anxiety, as with each new year, I had a different person to work with me, usually ignorant of autism and FC. Brenda, thank God, was always there for me. She tried to train these people to work with me, but they were just too ignorant, or didn't want to believe, so her efforts were in vain.

I did graduate last June from New Bedford High School, with honors, due only to Brenda and her undying loyalty and belief in me. She tutored me three nights a week and made sure I completed the required work. Without her, I never could have done it. And now we are in the same boat, trying to find someone to go to college with me.

In this respect, FC is like a two-headed dragon. In one respect, it opened a whole new world for me, a world in which I could attend public schools, could take and succeed in honors courses, could have some people look at me with respect and compassion in their eyes, could have some friends in school who really liked me for myself and look past the autism. Yet without someone to go to school with me who was trained in FC and the aspects of autism, I am lost.

It reminds me of that old question, "If a tree falls in the woods, does it make a sound?" What good is a "voice" if there is no one there to help facilitate its powerfulness? Will anyone be able to hear my voice? Will I be able to go to college? These are the questions I must ask myself now, and sit and wonder about, each day that I am at home instead of at school.

Yet, you are here today, and by being here, it shows me that you care about people with autism and the use of FC for them to be able to communicate with the world. You are hearing my voice, and I am asking you for help. We need more people like Brenda to work with us. I know there must be hundreds of children with autism whose entire lives could be changed if they were introduced to FC and had a dedicated person to work with them. We must somehow find people who would love to work with us and train these people. Especially in this area, the lack of trained facilitators is obscene, and something must be done.

FC is an earth shattering experience for anyone with autism. It enables you, in fact, to become a contributing member of society. It is a wondrous feeling to be looked upon as an intelligent person. FC gives you self esteem and pride in yourself that you never thought you would ever, ever have in this world. Your family also changes, because they, too, can now be proud of you and your accomplishments. FC brings much pleasure into your life and your family life, and even outdoor excursions become better because you can now voice your opinions on what to do, where to go, what you want to wear, and all of life's experiences, something that would be a definite impossibility without FC. But, we must be sure that there are enough trained, sensitive people out there to work with us all, for it can also be a frustrating experience to have this knowledge and intelligence and not be able to put it to any usefulness.

I will get off my band wagon now. I thank you for listening to me, and I hope there is someone out there who can help with the problem of too few facilitators in this area. Thank you all for coming today, you have renewed my hope that there still are people out there who really care about FC and us!

About the Author

Maegan Stoddard Gracia is a 23 year old young woman with autism. She graduated with Honors from New Bedford High School in 1999 using facilitated communication and assisted by an aide. Meg lives at home with her family. She has two sisters, Marcy and Angele, and one brother, Chip. She loves swimming, the beach and love stories. Her biggest thrill lately has been becoming an 'auntie' to nephew Bowen Michael.

Maegan is currently working on writing a book, *Strong on Hope*, which focuses on "communication as a behavioral truth." In the book, which is her own story, she also includes help for parents of youngsters with communication disorders like autism.

Maegan has presented at conferences and colleges, and is most interested in educating about autism and facilitated communication. "I'd like to continue my education and have made a vow to educate about autism and help others like myself."

Contact Maegan at PrdAut102@aol.com

Kenny celebrates his brother Derek's wedding

Kenny Affonce

Dare to Dream a Little Dream

Presented at the FC Conference, Autism Society of
America, Massachusetes Chapter, 1999

Nineteen years ago, when I was born, I'm sure my parents had
the same dream for me as they did for my older sister and
brother: that I would grow up to go to college and get a really
good job and live the American Dream. Then, when I was two,
disaster struck. I was diagnosed as being autistic, and if that
were not bad enough, I have a seizure disorder. As hard as it
was, I guess my parents had to let go of the dream they had
had for me, and try to concentrate on just getting me through
each day with as little difficulty as possible. My behaviors

were atrocious, and I'm sure it wasn't easy to deal with me on a daily basis. But my parents loved me, and they always tried to do what was best for me.

I attended several special needs programs in schools in the area - all segregated, non-inclusive schools. My behaviors did not improve; rather, they got worse from things I picked up from the other kids who were just as frustrated as I was. My father, being a very intuitive person, picked right up on this, and figured that if I could pick up bad behaviors, why couldn't I pick up on good behaviors, given the right role models? So he fought to get me included in a regular classroom in my neighborhood school. Even though I wasn't doing the same academic program as the other kids (I had my own one-to-one teacher, who worked with me on a preschool level), I was in my own school. They had also hired a behavioral psychologist to work on controlling my behaviors, and I was making some progress...but being in the classroom, hearing the teacher talking, understanding what she was talking about, knowing the answers to the questions but not being able to speak and communicate was the most frustrating experience I had ever had. This made my behaviors even worse.

Then that summer, a miracle happened! It came in the shape of a woman Dr. Weiss had hired to work with me at a summer camp program. She was hired to tutor me during the day. I would have half-a-day academics and half- a-day camp activities. We were still working with the same materials that I had been using in school, and naturally I was frustrated with this baby work. So at first my behaviors were still horrendous. The one big difference was that Brenda saw into my soul, and she knew there was a very bright little boy inside my body, desperately trying to get out. She knew I could read, she sensed that I understood everything going on around me, but that I just could not communicate with the world. She was as frustrated as I, trying to find some way for me to be able to communicate. Then she saw a program on facilitated communication (the first one, that was positive about what was happening), and she just knew we had to try it. It was very slow going at first, but Brenda did not give up, and soon I was able to communicate thoughts and feelings! How wonderful it is to be able to express myself! My behaviors improved so much that even Dr. Weiss, who was very skeptical, had to admit there was something there.

Well, that August, we presented my facilitated communication process to the Fairhaven School Board, and they agreed that I would start middle school with Brenda as my facilitator. That is when my parents could begin to dream again. I started sixth grade along with my friends from elementary school, but this time I was doing the same work they were. Not only that, I was doing it as well or better then they were! The kids were so happy for me, and it was the best experience of my life. I made many friends who have continued with me throughout high school. I have managed to maintain a place on the honor roll every semester I have been in school and was even inducted into the National Junior Honor Society when I was in middle school.

I am now in my senior year of high school, and even though we have had many difficulties— teachers who did not believe in F.C. and my many seizures and sicknesses—we have succeeded! I will graduate with my fellow students and friends, and the dream my parents have waited so long to see fulfilled will come true. I will go on to college, hopefully get a decent job, and live the American Dream! All of this was made possible by a little thing called facilitated communication and the hopes and dreams of my parents and a very special teacher. So please, when life seems without hope, remember my story, and dare to dream a little dream. No one knows what lurks behind a corner to be turned. Try new ideas, keep an open mind, and always, always have hope! I know it saved my life and made our dreams come true.

About the Author

In the time since this presentation was made, the life of Kenneth W. Affonce has gone through significant changes. Kenny obtained his high school diploma in June, 2000 with hopes of going on to college. On May 6th, 2001, his father, Ken, died after a battle with cancer. Kenny's father meant the world to him. After his father's death, he stopped facilitating with everyone.

Shortly after Ken died, Kenny turned 22, an important age for people with disabilities in Massachusetts. At this point they go from being funded by the school to being funded by a state agency, the Department of Mental Retardation. For a year Kenny continued to live with his family. Very few services were made available. His father Ken had been the person who knew how to "play the game" of getting services and Kenny's mother and brother, Derek, were not prepared for this responsibility.

After a year, Kenny moved into a group home. Derek is his legal guardian and is working to get Kenny the services he deserves and needs. Derek and Kenny are both very thankful for the help provided to the family by *The Nemasket Group* of Fairhaven, Massachusetts. As of August, 2003, Kenny is in a day program tailored to his needs that is run by The Nemasket Group, which is beginning to train its staff with FC to allow Kenny to regain his voice.

Kenny has not had a trained facilitator to work with him on a regular basis for two years. Through some of this time Ken, himself, chose not to use FC; at other times he had no one trained to facilitate him besides Derek and his mother. Although the "dream" was put on hold and the last few years have been difficult, there is light at the end of the tunnel. Kenny continues to have a goal of taking some college courses and maybe even pursuing a college degree, if funding allows.

Kenny would like to thank his father for being an innovator and fighting so hard to improve his life and give him a voice. The family would like to thank the people of The Nemasket Group for providing Kenny and his family with so much support

Kenny Affonce

and guidance through this voyage.

Contact Kenny at tacit@telusplanet.net

Jenn enjoys the scenery in Wales on her trip to England to promote Facilitated Communication

Jenn Seybert

Inclusion...Finally!!!

Keynote: Maryland Coalition for Inclusive Education
Baltimore, Maryland, 2002

My life without communication was 24 years of a living hell. Imagine yourselves sitting in your seats and having your thoughts constantly interrupted by thoughts of terror, your own voice sounding like a thunder of garbled words being thrown back at you, and other folks screaming at you to pay attention and finish your task. You find your body and voice do unusual things, and you realize you aren't in control. People are screaming at you to stop the aggression, and they stick a raisin or lemon juice in your mouth, depending on your response. Now add to this that you cannot talk...maybe a few words...but nothing consistent with language. With all this in mind, welcome to the world of a person with autism who is also non-verbal.

My life was always upside down. Nothing made sense. I kept trying to please but was not able to let anyone know what I was trying to say. We are a confusing lot. We are able to have intelligent brains, but our outward appearance is looked at as severely retarded. You are able to sit in your seats and have total control of your mind, voice and body. That isn't how we work. We are not in control all the time, and some of us folks, never. We want to comply, we want to please, but we can't make it work all the time.

You see, for the first 24 years of my life, my behavior was appalling, and I was aggressive, very unhappy, and always frustrated. Seven years ago I was introduced to facilitated communication, and my world became unlocked in an instant. That is when my whole life opened up and the hell of being locked inside of myself disappeared.

It wasn't easy to allow myself freedom from autism that holds you together like a cult. Opening my mind to healthy thoughts of life was very hard. We managed to work through issues as they came up. I struggled with how to tell good strategies from bad ones.

In the beginning I needed a lot of support, both emotional and physical. Like you, I will always want and need support from family and friends. My need for physical support, however, has been reduced to practically nothing at times. My thoughts are normal like yours, but my motor planning issue causes me to stall on each thought without the help of my facilitator to give me a gentle lift so I am able to get my next thought out.

You can see from my appearance that I look retarded. The motor planning issue I have to live with makes me not respond immediately. When you are talking with me, I appear to drift off or not be listening. I utter involuntary sounds or words. These issues are part of my inward battle. These issues I have to struggle to keep in control so that you, the audience, will believe in me as the author of my thoughts.

These are issues that many people contend with every hour of their lives. To those who are caregivers, teachers, case managers, parents, and staff, think of those people you support who have difficulty with communication and productive motor planning. Maybe you hadn't thought of their problems in that light before. Maybe you just thought "retardation" or "behavior problem."

In order for inclusion to succeed, it is of great urgency that you begin to look beyond our disability and really get to know us. Your views about our outward façade must change. To better understand what it means to be on the receiving end, let me share with you what it was like for me, growing up and going to school.

Unfortunately, until I went to college I did not have the opportunity to experience inclusive education. I would have benefitted greatly from this experience. On the other hand, because of my frustration in not being able to communicate my thoughts, the behaviors would have interfered with my being able to learn.

My group was taken out of our little world for the "specials," such as adaptive phys. ed., music, and, if we were having a good day, an assembly program.

As I grew up in the system, I felt like I might as well assume my role as retarded because this seemed my fate. I was given simple responsibilities, such as delivering notes to the office or taking the count to the cafeteria. I enjoyed the bits of freedom offered to me, so I made sure I did these well.

I "lucked out" during my years of being "educated"—if you want to call sequencing beads on a string and identifying penny, nickel, dime and quarter lucky! The teachers and aides were wonderful and, with their heart of hearts, did their job believing that what they were doing was helpful.

Learning to learn was and is a process for me as it is for everyone. It began with sitting and watching how others interacted. I also watched a lot of TV over the years, yes, many years of watching TV. My parents did make sure I was viewing something educational including nature channels, public television which broadcast Sesame Street, Carmen Sandiego, Bill Nye the Science Guy, and evenings of Jeopardy, Wheel of

Fortune and Star Trek.

While watching these shows or interactions between people, I seemed to be able to pull myself out of my dark world to process the information I was getting and to categorize and store it.

The way I learned was to watch and listen. I had a dear friend by the name of Herb Lovett, who was a psychologist and author to name a few of his many qualities, and he wrote about "Learning to Listen." This book touched me, because if educators and service workers would take the time to just watch and listen to us who are trying to share these thoughts with them, we could eliminate a great deal of confusion that exists.

Herb took the road of working with individuals in a positive manner, trying to discover what was causing the behavior and how to work through it. There was not a behavioral modification piece placed here, only listening and observing the person to work their issues through for their benefit.

All of us like to work with each other in a positive way, not talking in a loud and demanding tone with "rewards" attached to it. Even though I see the need for establishing limits, this can be done in a positive way.

But because I was not able to use any augmentative communication devices and could not speak without one, I lost out on 18 years of an education that could have formed the foundation for my life. My disability of autism was one that fell through the cracks, and I was always considered unique No one knew quite what to do with me. I harbor no blame or resentment, but I am on a mission to **educate** my audiences about my life so others in my situation can benefit.

In spite of my lack of education I was able to move forward with the help of those who believed in me. As the puppet in Pinocchio became, I am a real person. My new life with communication started out with forming a circle of support and developing a Person-Centered Plan. Here, I was encouraged to dream, share my wishes, and set my life in order. These folks listened, and as my goals were expressed, helped me to make the necessary changes to accomplish them. We met frequently because I was accomplishing goals as fast as I was setting them. Through this process another fact surfaced. Person-Centered Planning is and should be ongoing in an individual's life; as the person grows and moves forward, so does her goals.

The next step was to use my waiver dollars to accommodate my new life. That took work of developing a proposal and exploring my goals, but it paid off because, when living in Pennsylvania, I was among the first to be entrusted with self-determination dollars to manage. With the support now in place, I was able to go to college at Penn State, hire my companions and let them go, attend and present at conferences, and become a part of my community.

I began at Penn State by auditing one class. The next semester I audited another. The third semester I registered for two courses for credit. By the fourth semester, I applied as a provisional student, and I was accepted as a matriculated student by the fifth semester. It was difficult to be a college student because I did not have a formal high school background like my peers. It still remains a problem sometimes, but I do it.

A year ago we moved to central New York state and had to begin the process all over again. This was very difficult until we linked up with the right people who could make this come together for me.

All of my Penn State credits were accepted at Le Moyne College in Syracuse, and I am presently finishing up my second semester as a sophomore in the field of Psychology. I have been accepted by the faculty and my peers at Le Moyne and hope to continue on to graduate school for my Master's in Counseling. Each semester I take nine credits and am currently embarking on an internship. Along with my studies, I sit on a committee at the Facilitated Communication Institute that is involved in short and long-range research and planning. I am also creating my own inclusion path by joining organizations like the Psychology Club at Le Moyne. When an opportunity presents itself, I reach out to other non-verbal folks with autism who are going through rough times, continuing to encourage them to keep moving forward.

I have a companion who gives me several hours of fun along with a group of graduate students who I also meet with to socialize each Friday. My life is full and happy.

When you leave here today, please take my thoughts with you. Benefit others with them; reach out, and listen to those who sit in silence as their behaviors are saying something very important to you. Autism is not a death sentence, but not being able to speak does not mean we have nothing to say or cannot be included in social groups with other people.

When people are supported to emerge from behind the mask of "disability" and are able to reveal their true selves, they become the beautiful butterflies God meant them to be.

About the Author

Are you all aware of the benefits of hearing an individual who is using the augmentative process of facilitated communication (FC)? How I began this journey is quite a talk for me to share.

It began with the freeing from the darkness of autism, and adjusting to the outside world. I was so afraid but so excited to be able to share my thoughts and be listened to.

Then came the thousand questions by my family and friends. Then came my questions! A flood of feelings surfaced, and hurts I carried inside from things people said to me and about me became stumbling blocks for awhile until I sorted things out by communicating my feelings.

Opening myself up was difficult but cathartic. I will have autism forever, but sharing with families and professionals who are truly loving and caring feels good as I fill them with insight so they in turn can help their family member or people in their practice/classroom.

The next part of my journey was to benefit from Person-Centered Planning. Here the rubber hit the road and I really took off. I would sit with my circle of support and talk for hours on how I could get to a goal I would make. They would get so caught up in my excitement that they would forget I was there! I would accuse them of "yapping" and bring them back to the task at hand! Like as not we all had a great time, and I was in control. I could see my life evolving more and more, and the self-acutualizing was beginning to give birth inside of me.

I wanted to give presentations. I now have a resume three pages long of presentations. I wanted to vote; I now vote. I wanted to meet other individuals who use FC; I started a group called the Lonesome Doves.

Finally, but not last, as the last is yet to come, I wanted a college education, since I never got a high school one. I am presently a junior majoring in Psychology at Le Moyne College. I received a scholarship for the fall semester. This spring, I was inducted into Psi Chi Honor Society.

I have friends with whom I go to class. I have friends who are graduate students from Syracuse University, who I go out to "happy hour" with each Friday. I help with training at the Facilitated Communication Institute.

I, along with three fellow FC users, was invited to reintroduce FC in Bolton and Liverpool, England, this past May. It was awesome!

All of these experiences happened because I am able to use facilitated communication and make it work in my life. I feel I am still evolving and growing into the woman I was meant to become. I do not feel whole and complete because God is not done with me.

The journey of Jenn Seybert continues...

Contact Jenn at seyberjp@verizon.net

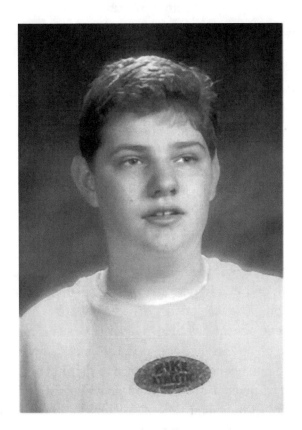

Jamie Burke

Life Is a Beach but Sometimes the Sands Hurt

Originally presented at TASH as the Keynote in Boston in 2002

Hi everyone! I'm Jamie Burke, and I hail from Syracuse, New York. I am being a very nice guy and won't deem to get really into the mode of preacher, but I want to tell you the truth in my life.

I have been a user of facilitated communication since a little boy of five small years. My mom was certainly wise when she made certain I was in a loving, inclusive school. I have not known any other way than that life of being assumed as an intelligent and able kid. My typing was so clear for the truths I felt and the choices I made. My voice was not useful. Speech, print and letters had always traveled on separate routes, never coming together to produce speech.

Finally, print, letters, and speech arrived together at the bus stop when I was twelve years old. I had seven lonely and frustrating years before my release from the silent sentence. My Lightwriter was the key in the jailhouse door. Now that I can speak, I feel very bold in believing that many of us who are locked into the silent world can be released through becoming familiar with our sensory avenues or differences and treating them with an array of therapies that give order and sense to our brains.

I continue to learn how to use my voice, and now I am in High School, and in a Regents Academic Program, and I am on the honor roll. The work is greatly tiring, but I am pleased to do it! I believe persons who have disabilities are considered to be assuming of no intelligence, and this makes my frustration explode as a mushroom cloud of atomic strength!

If you are given the choice to communicate, they can no longer live by that assumption. Of course, I am assuming they are intelligent enough to offer it!

I am seen as really oddball in the chances given to me to be considered intelligent. I have the joys of academics and the great things that bring feelings to me of hopes of college, dates, and jobs. I am saying this is the quest of everyone— good opportunities and fair chances. I wish my experience would not be that of an oddball, but that success as a person with autism would be evidence that others with disabilities can accomplish great things.

Today, I would like to share some thoughts on how all people with disabilities might be seen as worthy of success and opportunity. I see that people are like very lovely stones on a beach. You may walk along the sands, and see only one beautiful stone. Do not just pick that one up and think it's beautiful and the only one like it. All stones are worthy of being elevated from the beach. Remember that it took many years for that stone to become polished and smooth. It took many waves that were both wild and calm to make that stone shine. It takes a world of people to bring polish to the stone.

So my message to you, dear people, is become the waves, wash over the fears and the difficulties. You can smooth every rough edge of the sensory realm and bring a smooth way to gain entry to schools. To believe we are capable is to believe that the oceans are endless. The sands can be uncomfortable, but the waves, like the dedicated people who assist us, can make the rough smooth. The joy is immense. I am looked upon as a stone of beauty and worth.

You need to stroll your beaches in life and pick up those stones. Polish them with appreciation of their individual beauty and set them, not as a trophy of display, but invite others to share in the development, as it takes many, and I promise the world will not just have more decorations but useful lives and futures of worth!

About the Author

Jamie Burke is a 16 year-old sophomore at Westhill High School in Syracuse, New York. He is a fully included student in a Regents Academic Track program. Jamie has used facilitated communication since age five and has progressed from supported typing to independent typing and typing with two hands.

He has recently become able to read his typing out loud and to read unfamiliar text. Within the last three years, Jamie has begun to have useful and reliable speech. He is a frequent presenter at Syracuse University School of Education and has presented at numerous conferences throughout the United States and also in England.

In the Spring of 2001, Syracuse University produced a video written and narrated by Jamie, titled "Inside the Edge: A Journey to Using Speech Through Typing." This video won the

TASH Image Award for 2002, which honors those who challenge stereotypical beliefs of those with disabilities. Jamie is a regular attendee of Syracuse Symphony, enjoys reading, movies, vintage films, swimming, and bowling, and is a participant in the Young Actors Workshop of Syracuse Stage.

Contact Jamie at jgburke@syr.edu

Tyler Fihe

Understanding Autism: Why Inclusion Is So Important

Originally presented at the Maryland Coalition for Inclusive Education, in Baltimore, 2002

What do we need to understand about your communication and speech that would help you to be able to express yourself and be supportive of you?

I need to be given as many opportunities to communicate throughout the school day with as many people as possible. The problem that often happens is that I end up talking to my aide more than anyone else. I think the aide needs to help me learn how to initiate conversations with other people, because right now, I wait for her or others to initiate the conversation. I need to be taught how to do this, because it does not come naturally for me. I think if this hurdle could be overcome, it would make a giant difference in my life.

What do we need to understand about movement differences and what they mean?

Teachers need to understand that there are many movements and sounds I make that I have a difficult time controlling. Many teachers think at first that I'm doing these things on purpose, and that I am just too retarded to understand. What's missing here is their understanding. They need more education about autism and the movement differences that go with it. Teachers need to hear from individual students with autism to learn about their unique movement differences. This will really help pave the way toward better understanding.

What kinds of social relationships do you have and what do you want?

I have lots of students who say hi to me at school, but very few of them really take the time to get to know me. They are too busy talking to their verbal friends. The people I talk to the most are adults, because they are really interested in me right now. What I'd really like is to have a few students learn how to facilitate my communication, so I could be around students with no adults around. I'd also like to have a girlfriend, but I don't know if this can ever happen. I think the only way would be if she could help me with facilitation.

What is important about your school experiences in terms of helping you to learn and feel successful?

The thing that helps me learn and feel successful is being able to communicate to the world with facilitated communication. Without it, there would be very little opportunity for me to be included in regular education classes. There is no one else with autism this challenging in Santa Cruz included in junior

Tyler Fihe

high and high school classes, because they haven't learned to do facilitated communication. These students like me are all in segregated special day classes with limited ways of communicating. This form of communication is my liberation to a world of possibilities. Otherwise, I would exist in a prison of silence and sounds I can't control. This should tell you all what is most important for a person like me with autism.

About the Author

The truth shall set you free. Well, I've been telling the truth for a long time now, but freedom has not come yet. The desire to be able to talk like most people still exists, even though I have been expressing myself now through facilitated communication since I was six years old. Maybe if I could accept my form of communication, I wouldn't get so frustrated with this tedious way of speaking. Questioning skeptics add to my frustration. You'd think that after eleven years of facing doubting minds, I'd be quite good at handling this skepticism, but I'm still practicing with my detached attitude. When will this doubting community leave? When will the truth help others like me become free to talk and share their lives? These are the questions which continue to plague me every day.

I began communicating this way in first grade with my mother and with my school aide. This was very slow to be accepted by special education professionals. They just couldn't believe that someone like me could do this. I think this was one reason why it has taken me so long to learn how to type independently, because skepticism followed me year after year in elementary school, trying to wear down my spirit and stop my mother's ferocious determination. What no one realized was that the truth of my communication could not be stopped. We cannot stop because there is too much at stake.

Wasted lives without a way to communicate must no longer exist.

Where am I today in my life? I'm a senior at Santa Cruz High School in Santa Cruz, California. I will be taking Economics, Leadership, P.E., and a tutorial class for homework. I enjoy the students there. They have mostly gotten use to my different sounds and body movements. I am able to talk to them with the help of my wonderful school aide who supports me with Facilitated Communication on my Lightwriter. What is hardest for me now is living with two other guys with disabilities. I have been doing this for a year now, and it's supposed to help me learn to be more independent from my mother. There are some good things I'm learning there, but the most frustrating part is that none of the staff really knows how to do Facilitated Communication. This means that, when I'm there, I don't have my most effective way of communication. I resort to a few basic phrases that get me by, but in no way communicate what I'm thinking or feeling. It's one of the biggest frustrations in my life. You might best understand this if you try to communicate with only a few phrases for a week and see how this feels inside. Thank God, I've got my communication at school, so I don't go crazy. Then there's opportunities like this one where I get to share what's on my mind. This provides some relief, knowing that more people might hear my words and perhaps be changed somehow by this communication.

What this does is keep giving me hope that this form of communication will be tried with others, so that they too will see more possibilities for their lives to improve. When will the opportunities arise? This is what I long to know the most these days.

Contact Tyler at tyler_fihe@hotmail.com

Sharisa Joy Kochmeister

To Have a Voice
Is to Have a Choice

This speech was presented at the Graduate School of
Education at Denver University in February, 2003

*When disability, as race and gender before it, is examined
and illuminated, it can be seen beyond the personal misfor-
tune it is often claimed to be. If it is perceived as deviant,
compared to some prized norm arising from cultural expectations of how humans should look and act, it overwhelms the
person's other, less visible aspects.*
From "A Matter of Dignity" by Andrew Potok

Sharisa Joy Kochmeister

Whatever course you have chosen for yourself,
it will not be a chore but an adventure
if you bring to it
a sense of the glory of striving,
if your sights are set far above
the merely secure and mediocre.
David Sarnoff

Discovery consists of seeing
what everybody has seen
and thinking what nobody has thought.
Albert Szent-Gyorgyi

Even the stars in the heavens above us
are not what they appear to be!
Sharisa Joy Kochmeister

Many of you may not know me and may be wondering why I was asked to come here and speak to you today. Who, exactly, am I? First of all, my name is Sharisa Joy Kochmeister, but I prefer to be known as Sharisa Joy. What I would like to make clear, however, is not so much who I am or why I was asked to come, but why I chose to accept the invitation. The words you are about to hear were written by me as part of my ongoing effort to shatter the walls that separate me from you and us all from each other in so very many ways. I will be telling you a little about my life before and after I became able to communicate and about what inclusion on all levels has meant for me, because to me, inclusion should be an integral piece of EVERY aspect of all of our lives.

What amazes me is that some still call full inclusion a "fad." To my mind, this is merely their way of denying that it is the law in this country, both on federal and state levels. Sign language was also once considered a "fad," as were many currently popular treatments in such fields as psychiatry, psychology, medicine, etc.

Inclusion is here to stay – and so am I!!!!

One of my personal heroes, Helen Keller, once said: "One can never consent to creep when one feels an impulse to soar." I came here today because I feel that impulse so strongly, and because I spent many years creeping before my life opened up and I began to follow that impulse. I want to share that impulse to soar with as many people as I can because I know what it feels like to live without light and hope, and now I know how hope can free a person's spirit and mind.

"Hope arouses," as William Sloan Coffin, Jr., so eloquently put it, "as nothing else can arouse, a passion for the possible." What I have done in the past nine years was deemed by many to be impossible and has often been referred to as miraculous. I want to make it clear that neither it nor I are miracles. Both are possible because of extremely hard work and sheer force of will.

In coming this far from where I was and still conceivably could be, I focus on the words of the great American patriot, Thomas Paine, who stated: "The harder the conflict, the more glorious the triumph. What we obtain too cheap, we esteem too lightly; 'tis dearness only that gives everything its value."

When I decided that I was willing to work and fight my way out of my prison to freedom, I had to overcome evaluations that contained such pontifical statements as: "No hope! Uneductionable. No attention span. Her IQ is that of an infant. She should be institutionalized. She is and will *always* be incapable of communicating in any way." For pity's sake, what did they expect from a non-verbal, extremely withdrawn and abused child when they only used such indecently idiotic methodology as verbal IQ tests and observation of behavior in a self-contained special school? Just look around you anytime if you want to see people who would test poorly if all we chose to do was to observe their idiosyncratic, eccentric behaviors in environments that stifle individuality!!

When I was younger, people looked at me and often observed only an empty shell—a real "zero" in the greater scheme of things. When I began to communicate in October, 1991, this perception slowly began to change. In the years that have followed, I have changed also—quite dramatically. Given the opportunity to communicate, I began to shed the darkness that surrounded me. Ursula LeGuin, a great science fiction author, said it quite well in what sounds like such an accurate description of my breakthrough that I might have written it myself: "Imagine darkness. In the darkness that faces outward from the sun a mute spirit awoke."

Not only did my spirit and mind awaken, but they began to send out a wake-up call to all around me, a call that continues to emanate as I continue to progress. That call brought me into the light and brings me here today and will continue to propel me forward on an incredible journey through an unimagined and often unimaginable life. If this makes me a "hero" to some, I accept that role, because then I know I may be setting an example for others to follow. Trying to open minds is my life story. However, when someone's mind is padlocked and barred in ways that would defy Houdini, it often takes a miracle to get in. But even if I'm not a miracle, I still believe in them, so I guess I'll keep trying to shatter those bars, pick those padlocks and open those tightly shut minds.

Because I am still almost entirely unable to speak, I am forced to *slowly* type all of my thoughts and feelings, even the most private ones. Although typing has shattered countless walls for me, it is still a torturously slow process, and there are many days I would gladly give up my legs for the opportunity to speak the messages of my mind and heart and soul. I do not, however, have this option, so I rely on typing as my "enabler." It allows me to communicate with and exist in a world where I once was and would otherwise still be a total stranger. It permits me to prove I am alive, smart, and able to think, understand, feel, hope, plan, hurt and dream just like the "verbalizers" of this world. I LOVE getting strong reactions of delight, realization, surprise or shock, and know that what I've said is meaningful and important and has made an impact. I cause people to think and help them to change and grow. I make them forget what they already believe they know and alter their previously learned perceptions of disability and reality. I thus accomplish my greatest goal—being an instigator for change and growth. Some would refer to me as a revolutionary of sorts. At best, I will admit to the fact that what I'm doing with my life and plan on continuing to do is very revolutionary for a person with my types and severities of disabilities. For me, however, it's the *only* choice I have in order to remain true to my own conscience and the inner voice that makes me who and what I am.

Since I began to communicate via typing, I have shattered many walls, both inside myself and in the world around me. I've had to overcome many prejudices, both from others towards people with disabilities as well as my own towards those who don't have any labeled disabilities. I've had to fight for the right to the education I'm supposedly guaranteed by law; for the opportunity to be heard by the legal system; and for the chance to overcome the beliefs of many skeptical and cynical individuals within the media and the medical and educational communities. This has taken tremendous energy and incredible intestinal fortitude, in addition to a streak of sheer stubborn determination not to let anyone get the better of me or return me to the life in which I had been trapped.

When I first started to type, I had already spent in excess of eleven years with no effective means of communication. I couldn't nod, speak, or use sign language effectively because of my "dyspraxia." I compare dyspraxia to inertia. I do so because inertia, as I understand it, is the inability to move unless something else makes it possible. I easily relate to this. Dyspraxia is best defined in laymen's terms as an inability to make one's muscles do what one wants without great difficulty or assistance. Sometimes it makes me "freeze in my tracks" or "forget" how to move, walk, chew, or swallow. It makes it difficult to do something as seemingly simple as nodding my head or shaping my fingers for sign language or walking downstairs alternating feet or using my eye muscles properly or my mouth, tongue, throat and facial muscles to speak clearly.

I had also learned how to live *down* to expectations of

others, including teachers, medical and therapy professionals, so-called friends, and family. People totally believed that I was "hopelessly retarded" because I couldn't express myself or respond in any acceptable way... and to all outward appearances, that's exactly what I was... but NOT BEING ABLE TO SPEAK IS **NOT** THE SAME AS NOT HAVING ANYTHING TO SAY!!!!

When I finally started communicating, the "communication chasm" I had to cross was so wide, I needed to take a "quantum leap" merely to begin the long journey upon which I was about to embark. Comparable to my leap, but seemingly far more difficult to achieve, is the one other people had to make (and often still do) to believe in me. How exactly did I prove myself? When I started typing, numerous "experts" in communication, education, psychology, and neurology refused to believe the words were my own. They forced me to prove myself time and again, through tremendously upsetting, anxiety-provoking formal and informal tests specifically designed to prove that people doing what I did were not really the ones communicating.

Despite their best efforts, I passed every test thrown at me both with and without physical support. In spite of the extensive damage to my psyche, I somehow managed to overcome all of this and become the person I am today – respected by others for my victory against enormous odds and the subject of countless anecdotes, media reports and even documentaries.

People should never be seen or treated as labels. I refuse to be pigeonholed by my disabilities, and my continued success ensures that I will not be. And yet, some people would still prefer to see me return to my world of silent darkness. Why, oh why can't these fools just allow us "non-verbal" people to be people rather than trying to depict and keep us as some kind of non-communicative, unthinking, unfeeling "vegetables?" It's good to know that people can change their perceptions through exposure to new people and concepts. It is, nevertheless, sad that some people go through life with the blinders and earplugs of prejudice so firmly in place. It's even worse when they try to impose those beliefs on society; innocent people get irreparably hurt.

While I know that not all people with autism are mentally retarded, in my own case and in some others, there is/was a level of functional retardation that delayed me as well as a motor planning disorder and cerebral palsy which tended at times to make me appear "retarded" in behavior and affect. I feel deep personal shame about having acted retarded to live *down* to expectations, even though it was the safest thing for me at that time. Even today, as an accepted third year student in a very difficult private university, there are times my behaviors and affect might cause people who don't know my true intelligence to think I seem "retarded." The only answer I can see to this type of tunnel vision is to attempt to educate others to see past surface behaviors and not to make a blanket assumption of incompetence when true competence might indeed be present. The benefit of the doubt is often the best gift we humans can give to other humans... I've even learned to give it to people I consider to be "attitudinally challenged."

Truly, my father and I have been through hell and back in trying to fight for my rights. And the fight just *never* seems to totally end, especially in light of the fact that the State of Colorado has refused to provide me with services for the developmentally disabled. They have declared that I am not developmentally disabled because their "experts" found my intelligence levels to be far too high on tests that I took independently in November, 2000!!! For pity's sake, I was classified as developmentally disabled in New York. Did moving 2000 miles somehow magically change that? So what if my IQ is too high? What about my many deficits and needs for total assistance in the areas of daily living and survival skills as a result of several disabling conditions which are classified as developmental disabilities under federal law? It seems that one needs to be retarded in this state just to be able to get on waiting lists for necessary services, or is, perhaps, the system retarded that sets up IQ or lack of it as a measure of developmental disability and need? I have to wonder at the motives of people who challenge either my intelligence or my disabilities... exactly what do they want me to be? I have already jumped through countless firey hoops to get to where I am today. I am sick and tired of being treated as a human guinea pig or lab rat. It is a clear violation of my human rights and one that *must* stop *now!* What exactly will I be asked to prove next—that I am actually HUMAN????!!!! YEESH!!!! Enough of my anger at the flawed system. I promised you all that I would talk about inclusion, so here is my personal experience with it.

Since I began communicating in 1991, I've taken many difficult and dangerous leaps in order to conquer walls in such tricky areas as independence, emotional maturity, socialization skills, and trust. What was probably my most difficult leap was from "retarded" school to accelerated seventh grade classes in a regular junior high school. And one short year later – high school, which I finished in a mere three years! High school was, indeed, a learning experience on EVERY level and for everyone involved. I had to modify what others regarded as bizarre behavior in order to fit in with my peers, be accepted by my teachers and administrators, and not get kicked out of classrooms, which happened more than once, or suspended from school, which actually happened once. I also had to manage to stay true to myself while doing this, a daunting task for anyone, to be sure. That I did so, and still managed to become seen as a role model, win academic and social awards, become a published author, performed songwriter, acclaimed public speaker, and honors graduate (3.9+ cumulative average) is testimony to my sheer force of will when it comes to proving myself and maintaining my individuality at one and the same time.

I received President Clinton's award for "Significant Community Service" at my high school graduation, and was also commended by New York State's Developmental Disabilities Planning Council and the New York State Self-Advocacy Society for my advocacy efforts on behalf of people with disabilities. I passed the college English Entrance Exam with high honors and was the only incoming student at SUNY Rockland ever to be offered an Independent Learning Contract in Freshman Writing because my score was so high, and they felt that my writing skills were already so finely honed! In the fall of 1997, I leapt into college at SUNY Rockland and have been almost a straight A student thus far for five years at both Rockland and Denver University, despite initial obstacles such as the need for extended time and a quiet setting for testing. Sadly, when I got straight A's on my first several tests without a proctor, certain cynical, skeptical fools once again assumed that my father might be doing the work instead of me. We both found this almost laughable, because he was never better than a B student in high school or college and I graduated high school with honors and an A+ average. I'm very proud to say that all tests subsequently proctored resulted in A's, and I now almost invariably take my tests in the classroom in full view of professors and classmates... and do even better, often finishing before many other students and getting A's and A pluses on nearly every exam I've taken since.

I have been both the victim of twelve years of total exclusion and four years of so-so inclusion in education and the extremely happy and fortunate beneficiary of in excess of five years of superior inclusion in college. I publicly praise my colleges, the State University of New York at Rockland and the University of Denver for treating me with respect and dignity and making me feel welcome, successful and fully included as a member of both the academic and social communities. I've neither asked for nor received preferential treatment, and I enjoy being viewed as and treated almost exactly like every other student in both regular and honors program classes, with a few brief exceptions to this rule... for instance, they say I bring up the test curve in my classes and inspire other students to do better, and several times I've even been asked to guest lecture my classes. I have gained greater self-esteem, self-confidence and pride, enabling me to achieve beyond even my own original high expectations and internal standards. My professors and classmates befriend and accept me as the person I am, eccentricities and all. They no more expect me to conform to their behavior than I expect them to conform to mine. We are learning from each other, and that's the way it should be!

I have been a member, secretary, vice-president and president of the Political Science/Pre-Law Association, a writer for the student newspaper, *The Outlook*, a contributing writer, member of the editorial staff and co-editor-in-chief of the college literary magazine, *Impulse*, at SUNY Rockland, and was chosen for *Who's Who in American Junior Colleges*. In March of 1998, during my freshman year, I was chosen to represent Rockland at a prestigious conference at the Center for the Study of the Presidency in Washington, D.C. My attendance as the only student there with a noticeable disability was a disturbing surprise to me, just as I'm sure that I was a surprise to those who met and spoke with me.

After all, most of the verbalizers of this world never even come into contact with a person who needs to use a keyboard device to communicate. In this very impatient society of ours, few people seem to have the time to wait for me to finish expressing myself through slow, one-fingered typing before they leave my presence. Yet there I was and here I am on my continuing incredible odyssey. All this and I'm still only twenty-four! It gets more amazing every day just being me!

Shortly thereafter, I was one of a select group of fifty young people with disabilities chosen from many hundreds of applicants to participate in government-sponsored leadership training in June of 1998 in Washington once again. This time, I actually got to meet President Clinton by invitation at the White House (before the Lewinsky scandal, thank goodness!) and have my photo taken with him and with Senator Tom Harkin (sponsor of the IDEA) when I ate lunch at the Senate Office Building. Despite all these amazing and prestigious events, however, I'd have to say that the single coolest thing that happened in my career at SUNY Rockland occurred in May of

1999 when I was chosen to receive an "Outstanding Student Service Award" for my extracurricular accomplishments by my fellow students and professors. I was honored at a luncheon and awards ceremony at which I was the *featured* honoree and was asked to deliver a speech to everyone present... including my friends and family!   My reaction at receiving such a prestigious award from my *peers* could best be summed up in one word – OUTSTANDING!!!!

I received my Associate's Degree in Humanities and Social Sciences with honors from SUNY Rockland in May of 2000, and in September of 2000 I began the rather brave excursion of being a transfer student at Denver University, majoring in Cognitive Sciences and minoring in English. My GPA for first quarter was 4.0, and I set the curve on both the midterm and final exams in my Psychology of Learning course. Second quarter I took Cognitive Neuropsychology and Literature and Music in the Jazz Age. I had to withdraw from third quarter classes because of a very nasty intestinal illness which kept me hospitalized for nearly four weeks in March and April, but I returned to school in the summer and got A's in Psychology and Mythology classes. I have changed my major to Psychology and my minor to Sociology and have done very well in the 01-02 and 02-03 academic years despite more illnesses that curtailed my schedule somewhat.

The courses I take, the people with whom I interact, the lessons I learn—all combine to enrich my life and broaden my horizons and expand my goals.

I believe that, within reason, there is *nothing* I can't do if I really set my mind to it. The future is open and bright before me and all I really need to be is ME!

My original post-college plan was law school. It was my ambition to be a Human Rights attorney and judge—until I decided that I disliked lawyers way too much to ever become one of them. Now I'm well on my way to my new goal of being a neuropsychological researcher and winning a Nobel Prize for brain injury research; and better yet, I love every minute of it!! I may or may not fulfill those goals, I may or may not change my mind about my career, I may or may not marry and have kids, but ultimately I will do anything my heart desires and to which I aspire... ultimately, that's all up to me, just as it should be to *everyone!*

What I try to carry everywhere I go is my own unique example of what might lie behind what people think they see if they will only open their eyes, ears, hearts, minds and souls to what is *truly* possible. As I tell everyone, people only need to be themselves and allow themselves to really get to know me in order for me to feel comfortable enough and safe enough and trusting enough and emotionally secure enough to be myself and allow myself to know them. I'm also very lucky that I can hear and extremely fortunate to have communication devices of my own that enable me to "speak." I believe these should be made available to all people with communication and/or hearing impairments. They should be equipped with voice output in a variety of voices as well as visual and/or printed output in case the person to whom you are communicating also has a hearing impairment. Children should be given them and trained in how to use them at the earliest age possible, and similar training should be provided to their family members, peers, teachers, and all other caregivers who work with them. It is hard enough to live in silence without anybody or anything making it harder or more uncomfortable in any way. Technology, education, inclusivity, increased awareness, and understanding are the best answers to making disabilities such as these less disabling. The only *real* answer is to enable; anything less only disables. I can state unequivocally that anyone who is denied these opportunities is denied both the right to communication of their own and a life that surpasses any they might have without that communication.

Socrates believed that "*The way to gain a good reputation is to endeavor to be what you desire to appear.*"

Henry Miller said: "*Example moves the world more than doctrine.*"

Paul G. Hawken states that: "*We lead by being human. We do not lead by being corporate, professional, or institutional.*"

B.C. Forbes believed that: *"Difficulties should act as a tonic. They should spur us to greater exertion."*

These days, I have unlearned most of my autistic-like behaviors and am much more open and friendly, can act with more decorum, and continuously try to overcome my terror of trusting in order to let more people into my world. College has helped me learn to do this more and more. These past few years have been, for me, a time of awesome ADVANCES! Many incredible things have happened and continue to happen in my life, and the question of how I continue to do and accomplish things has been asked of me and by me again and again. Many of these advances were accompanied by excruciating effort, struggle, anguish, anxiety, fear, and pain. Others have been accompanied by amazing hope, joy, triumph, pride, and a super sense of accomplishment. It is my goal to continue on the latter path.

My particular roads were by no means well-beaten paths. In fact, there were many times I knew I was the first and possibly the only traveler ever to use these particular, peculiar byways upon which I suddenly found myself. While I was, in one sense, like the famous astronaut, Neil Armstrong, setting his feet on the previously pristine surface of the moon, I was also quite unlike him by virtue of the fact that I had no one at all to observe my small steps or soften my large falls. During the past few years, however, my audience has finally arrived and my fellow travelers have, at long last, appeared and increased. They continue to do so, and my perilous pathways and hazardous highways continue to merge into smooth, straight, safe superhighways that lead me to the strangest of places that I never expected to visit! What's even stranger is that those strange places are beginning to look and feel just like "home" to me.

I can't help but wonder what intrepid, intricate and intriguing turns my journey will take in the years ahead.

It has been an amazing roller-coaster ride, but at least these days it is mostly fun instead of frightening, and I believe the trend will continue in that direction!

I fervently hope that someday, when people look back at me as a classmate, a speaker and presenter, or whatever other role I may yet play in this life, they will reflect not on the strangeness of my disabilities but on my excellent reputation, the examples I set, the uniqueness of my humanity, my ability to overcome my own barriers as well as those of society, and the impact my presence has had on each of them and their lives. That is certainly how I will think about all of the people with whom I come in contact in my life.

Thank you all for listening today and for trying to see and accept me as not just an expert or an anomaly, but as a real person. Thank you also for joining me on this leg of my journey and allowing me to share my gifts with you and permitting me to continue to explain and educate!

About the Author

My name is Sharisa Joy Kochmeister. I am 25 years old, and my disabilities include autism, epilepsy and cerebral palsy with severe motor planning difficulties. I used to be considered "profoundly retarded" and am now considered to be a "genius." I am, however, still almost entirely nonverbal and communicate via the use of keyboard devices. None of these is, however, nearly as important as the fact that I'm a senior at Denver University, about to graduate with an A- average, a published author, performed songwriter, and a member of *Who's Who In American Junior Colleges*. The latter was based on receiving my associate's degree in Humanities and Social Sciences from SUNY Rockland with honors in June, 2000, along with winning an Outstanding Student Service Award for being president of the Political Science-Pre-Law Association, writer and editorial staff member of the literary magazine, and staff writer for the newspaper.

I've also won state and national advocacy awards, including one from President Clinton, one from the New York State Developmental Disabilities Planning Council, and one from the New York State Self-Advocacy Society. I've taken part in many important conferences and symposiums, both nationally and internationally, as a speaker and presenter and have been invited to many places to speak publicly about my life and about issues surrounding disabilities, inclusion, and human rights. I did a keynote speech in Sacramento, California, in September of 1999 before 1600 people for the California Supported Life Institute's 13th annual conference, and since moving to Colorado in June, 2000, I have continued my public speaking and advocacy efforts before such groups as the Colorado Developmental Disabilities Planning Council, The Arc, The Colorado State Speech-Language-Hearing Association, Denver University and others. I keynoted and presented a workshop to all 120 directors of special education for the state of Colorado in May, 2001, was part of an expert panel on autism for the Kentucky Autism Training Center's Autism Institute in June, 2001, and was keynote speaker at an autism conference in Houston in June, 2002. To tell the truth, however, the best reward for me these days is neither praise nor awards nor speaking engagements nor even A's in my courses, believe it or not, but rather the knowledge that I help others and educate people to see beyond disabilities to the possibilities of the person within. All I really want is, insofar as possible, to be treated almost exactly like everyone else. Technology, education and full inclusion are the keys. The only real answer is to enable; anything less only disables.

You can reach Sharisa at SHARISAJOY@comcast.net

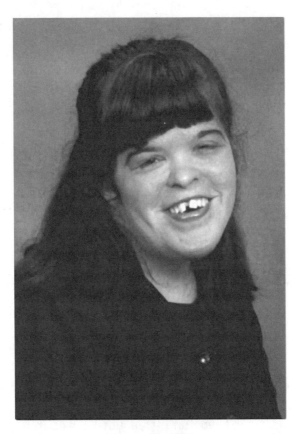

Sue Rubin

Facilitated Communication: The Key to Success for a Nonverbal Person with Autism

Keynote: presented at the Autism Society of America
2003 National Conference

My name is Sue Rubin and I am glad to be here today to tell you about my life and facilitated communication. Typing is very slow, so I have prepared my talk at home. When my facilitator has finished reading it, I will answer questions so you can see how I type to communicate. I know many of you may have read that facilitated communication is a hoax and that the facilitator was the person communicating. I hope this story of my life will change your mind. We people who use facilitated communication all have interesting stories, and mine is just one of many.

The story I am about to tell you sounds fantastic, but I can assure you it is true. I can also assure you that many people with autism who use FC are also having life-changing experiences. My own story starts with a very autistic child who was quite aggressive toward others—biting, pulling hair, throwing my head against someone's body, etc. I was also self-abusive—head banging, throwing myself against walls, biting, and quite ready to throw myself on the ground. I was so autistic that I was in a separate world. When I was four, my IQ was 50, but as I got older, the score went down, so by the time I was 13, my IQ score was 24. When I took these tests, I was totally unaware of what was expected of me. The tester spoke to me, but she quite sadly could have been speaking a foreign language. Sounds always went over my head, and I definitely wasn't able to complete any tests. Fortunately, we no longer have to depend on IQ tests when we want to see how smart a person is.

From the time I was an infant until I was in high school, I went to severely handicapped special education classes on regular school sites and was mainstreamed into regular science and other classes. The intention was social, but I was also exposed to grade level curriculum. My own special education curriculum was functional because no one thought an academic curriculum would be useful or even possible for me. Not only did I have horrendous behavioral problems and lack of language, I was awash in autism and totally dependent on behavior modification to get me through the day. The speech therapists tried everything they knew to get a communication system working for me. I couldn't even use a system based on pictures because I couldn't point or select pictures properly. Behavior was my only method of communication, and that got pretty ugly sometimes. Whittier was always in the forefront of special education, and I don't want you to think I had an awful educational program. We lived behavioral mod and positive behavioral supports. We practiced finding antecedents, behavior and consequences. My school records are loaded with functional analysis. However, I was still a mess.

In 1991 when I was thirteen and in an eighth grade severely handicapped class, the school psychologist and speech therapist contacted my mom and suggested trying facilitated communication with me. My mom had heard about the ouija board affect and had read negative things about FC. She said she didn't want them to try it, but they were so persistent, she agreed, and they came to my house. I was as amazed as they were when I could spell parts of words with someone pulling back on my wrist. The speech therapist was successful with all of the students in my SH class, as was the classroom teacher. The teacher typed with me at school everyday, and my mom typed with me at home. I slowly progressed from single words to phrases and sentences and paragraphs. During this time it became apparent that I had been learning from the mainstream classes and my older brother's homework and had been storing the information in my head. My brain was so disorganized that it took months for me to be able to organize information and retrieve it. It took even longer for me to be able to clearly express original thoughts, not just short answers to homework.

When the year was over, we decided I should go to Whittier high school where they already had a full inclusion program. The difference now was that I would be taking academic classes toward a regular diploma. We chose honors and advanced placement classes to avoid taking classes with a lot of cooperative learning and behavior problems of non special ed students. We started with three classes and worked up to five classes each day. The transition to high school was very difficult for me, and I often had to be removed from class. The psychologist was on call and often rushed to the high school when I was having a melt down. I really believe that being in regular classes and having to spend hours doing homework everyday and on the weekends was what enabled me to overcome a lot of the autistic behaviors I was constantly battling. After a while it became easier and easier for me to stay in class. I became relaxed and spent less energy fighting autism.

By the time I graduated high school I was a thinking person. I was sadly still autistic but no longer living in a separate world. I was quite aware of current events and aware of the thoughts and feelings of my peers and family. Because I was doing grade level work with few accommodations and earned a high school diploma with honors, I was able to apply to college. With a 3.98 GPA and 1370 on my SATs, I was accepted to Whittier College, a private, small liberal arts college quite close to home. Today I am a junior and a history major. Because I only take one or two classes each semester, it will take me several more years to graduate. I love learning and have thoroughly enjoyed my classes. The professors have been wonderful and enjoy having me in class. Professors I have had and others who have heard about me have asked me to take their classes. They like me because I always am prepared for class and participate a lot with ideas a little different from most students.

When I graduated high school, I wanted to leave home like my brother did, so my parents bought me a house near campus where I live with support from an adult agency. My support staff at school and at home are all people my age who have been taught facilitated communication. When I am at school or in the community, I type without physical support, but I still need a facilitator to keep me focused. Of course, at school the facilitator also takes notes for me and serves as a study partner when I am preparing for tests. The only accommodation I have is extra time on papers and tests. I have been doing well at school and have an A- average. I was recently inducted into Phi Alpha Theta International Honor Society in history.

This is not as fantastic or unusual as it might seem when you realize that I am the product of a school district that includes FC as an Augmentative and Adaptive Communication (AAC) method when assessing a student's needs. In Whittier, we have about 100 students with various labels doing grade level work using FC. In the adult world we have at least 30 people in the agency that supports me using FC everyday in colleges, home or the community. Other agencies in the Whittier area also use FC for their non-verbal and limited verbal consumers.

I certainly don't want you to think that the only success I have had is academic. Facilitated communication has enabled me to form friendships with my staff who are my peers. I now am able to nominate who will be a friend and who will remain just a staff member. I interview potential staff members and decide who I will have WAPADH, the adult agency, hire. I also decide who I want to fire if I don't like the way they relate to me. The people who I decide should become my friends do so because I have friendship to offer them in return. This would be impossible without facilitated communication. We are truly friends, and although they are actually staff members, they spend a lot of time with me when they are not being paid. We go dancing at clubs, visit museums, do outdoor things, and really enjoy going to Vegas. We are upscale young adults who enjoy spending time together. I know that if I were still living at home, I would not be nearly as independent as I am with my peers. My parents are very nice, but they are too old to do the things we do as friends. Having friends is the best part of my life. I really can't express to you how wonderful it is to have real friends who respect me in spite of my autism. I know they would be kind to me if I couldn't communicate, but they certainly wouldn't be friends. We discuss all sorts of things and excel at gossip.

Although they get excellent, awesome, really good salaries and are exceptional people, I know that they would not remain my friends if I still exhibited the horrendous behavior I did when I was a child. Because of Facilitated Communication, I was able to participate in my own behavior plans when I was in high school. I also wrote my own social stories to address specific situations. Although I still am quite able to throw a terrible fit, they are very few and far between. I can communicate with my staff when something is bothering me, and we can avoid a tantrum. Very simply, without FC I would be an object of pity rather than a friend. It is essential that a non-verbal person be able to express what is causing a behavior. Sometimes it is neurological, and there is no reason. In that case, I just ask them to keep me safe until it passes. Other times, there is something that triggers the behavior, and we can discuss what we can do to prevent a tantrum. The ability to tell when you are sick is extremely important. The awful behavior I sometimes had was a reaction to ear infections. I still get them but can tell staff I have to go to the doctor.

If FC is so beneficial, why aren't more school districts and adult programs embracing it? I would like to pose some possible reasons. First of all, we look retarded, especially when we move around. Some of us with motor planning problems have pervasive movement problems. Our bodies just won't do what we want them to do. We look retarded when we can't respond to commands. Secondly, by admitting FC works, most professionals alive today would have to admit they were very wrong about 75% to 80% of us having mental retardation. Thirdly, if school districts and adult agencies admitted FC works, they would be ethically obligated to completely change their programs. I also believe that many professionals feel threatened that people who look and act like us could be smarter than they are.

I have touched on the technique of FC a little and would like to go into it with more detail. I think most nonverbal people with autism can learn FC with a patient and well-trained facilitator. The people we see at our monthly workshops, where I teach, are progressing much faster than I did because we have better facilitators now. The goal of FC is for the person to type without physical support. It took me five years of gradually fading support to become independent. Now some people who have minimal motor planning problems can become independent in a few months when making choices on a dry erase board and totally independent soon after.

When a person begins FC training, she sometimes has a working brain and just needs a way to express herself. This type of person learns FC quickly. If the person is like I was and absolutely awash in autism, it takes a bit longer. We start with support at the wrist if the person can isolate a finger. We immediately move support up the arm so the person doesn't become dependent on a lot of support. The facilitator never guides the user, but rather pulls the arm back to a neutral position above the target whether it is a keyboard or pictures. The facilitator might also intermittently take a hand away so the person feels he is able to do it with minimal support. The facilitator starts with simple yes and no questions, then moves to predictable answers, then answers with a few choices, and finally open-ended answers. The goal is not only to be able to type without support, but to think and generate original thoughts. Copying words may be a good exercise for the facilitator to teach a person how to use a keyboard, but it is not really communication. Typing echolalia is actually harmful because it interferes with a person's ability to have original thoughts. Even when a person can do this independently, it should be discouraged. Also, when a person speaks echolalia and types it, he should be told not to speak because it is preventing him from developing sophisticated thoughts. When he stops talking, you will see the content of his typing change. This is very difficult for the FC user because he is used to using the automatic part of his brain, and you are asking him to turn that off and use the thinking part of his brain.

To become a good facilitator, you must read about it, attend workshops, and have a mentor to be sure you are doing it right. If you live in an area where there are no good trainers, you might want to use video tapes and have a trainer critique your work. You must be careful that you are not influencing the person typing. I recommend looking at the Facilitated Communication Institute's web site at Syracuse University http://soeweb.syr.edu/thefci. You can download the Facilitated Communication Training Standards and also purchase books and video tapes on FC. The standard training book for the method is *Facilitated Communication Training* by Rosemary Crossley.

The scientific proof of facilitated communication being valid already exists. I recommend that you read the August, 1996, study by Cardinal, Hanson and Wakeham in *Mental Retardation*, 34(4),231-242, in which 75% of the 43 subjects in the study validated their ability to pass a message to a naive facilitator using FC. In this study, only answers that were spelled perfectly were counted as correct. I have attached a list of the studies where FC users have validated their typing. There are also studies that show FC doesn't work. If you are interested in finding out why some studies have shown it doesn't work and others have shown it does, I recommend a book by Doug Biklen and Don Cardinal called *Contested Word, Contested Science: Unraveling the Facilitated Communiciation Controversy.* After examining all of the studies in print at the time, both positive and negative, Biklen and Cardinal found fourteen elements that had to be present in sufficient amounts for the FC user to pass a test successfully:

1. Extensive experience with facilitation by both the facilitator and the user
2. Practice using multiple trials
3. Facilitated communication user consults on test and format
4. Familiar facilitators
5. Monitoring for FC user's style
6. No-risk or low-risk testing
7. Building confidence
8. Naturally controlled conditions
9. Ongoing feedback on performance
10. Minimization of word retrieval tasks
11. Information by multiple modalities
12. Age-appropriate content
13. Personally relevant content
14. Extensive time to respond to questions

I believe the most important element is number 2—practice using multiple trials. In the Cardinal study, all students failed the tests the first day. If that had been the end of the study, it would have been one more study proving FC doesn't work; however, because the study was conducted with multiple trials over six weeks, students became comfortable with the protocol and were able to answer the questions. Because we saw what happened with this study, we used that information when I was preparing for the SAT. I spent the whole summer doing practice tests, so when I took the real SAT, I only had to think about the answers, not about taking the test.

The most troubling aspect of FC for some school districts and adult agencies is the fear of abuse allegations made by FC users. I understand this; however, what most people don't know is that only one study has been done looking at abuse allegations using FC, and that study concluded that such allegations should be taken seriously because so many had corroborating evidence. Here is the reference for the entire study: Botash, A., Babuts, D., Mitchell, N., O'Hara, M., Manuel, J., & Lynch, L. (1994). Evaluations of children who have disclosed sexual abuse via facilitated communication. *Archives of Pediatric Medicine*, 148, 1282-1287.

This being said, I must also warn you that all allegations of abuse, or actually, any allegation should be taken seriously only if there is reason to believe an incident has taken place. Not only is it possible for a facilitator to influence a person either physically or by asking leading questions, but it is quite possible that the FC user is lying or has confused a created scenario with reality. I have done both of these things—the first when I was testing the people around me, and the second when I honestly did confuse scenarios in my imagination with reality. This being said, I am still adamant about a person having the right to communicate in spite of the dangers involved in FC. The wonderful life I lead now, which I thoroughly enjoy, would not be possible without facilitated communication. The changes in my behavior, the changes in my relationships with family and friends, and the growth and maturity I have gained have been worth a bit of caution. The ability to communicate is definitely a civil right, and you should be obligated to assure that right is extended to your children and students.

About the Author

Sue Rubin was born May 25, 1978, and was diagnosed as developmentally delayed as an infant. At the age of four, she was diagnosed with autism and moderate mental retardation and was educated in Special Day Classes with some degree of integration until high school. Over time she continued to test at the 2 to 2 1/2 year level, which was compatible with her limited expressive and receptive language and the way she moved her body. By the age of thirteen, she still scored at this level, which to all appearances was correct. She was (and is) highly echolalic, obsessive/compulsive, has rages or tantrums, is self abusive and aggressive. In spite of this, Sue is a student at Whittier College, having graduated with honors from Whittier High School as a fully included student, with a 3.98 GPA and 1370 on the SAT. She holds a John Greenleaf Whittier Scholarship ($38,000) awarded solely on merit, without regard to her disability; carried the 1996 Olympic Torch as a Community Hero in Los Angeles; received CALTASH's 1st Annual Mary Falvey Outstanding Young Person Award in 1998; has presented at over 50 conferences, workshops, and classes; was the subject of two KCET (Los Angeles' public T.V. station) *Life and Times* programs; had two articles published in the *L.A. Times*; two articles published in *TASH Connections*; was the recipient of the 1999 Wendy F. Miller Outstanding Individual with Autism Award presented by the Autism Society of America; was the principal author of an article in *Disability and Society*; and was recently elected to the National Board of Directors of TASH.

Sue Rubin

Sue, a dedicated advocate for people with disabilities, presently has a 3.7 GPA at Whittier College and works as a consultant to WAPADH, an adult agency, on issues of communication, supported living, and behavioral interventions. She lives off-campus, with support.

Sue would be happy to receive your comments and questions. Reach her at srubin693@earthlink.net

Wallace Wojitowicz, Jr.

The Essence of Facilitated Communication

Presented in 1998 at the *Direct Service Conference* sponsored by the Maine Department of Mental Health, Mental Retardation & Substance Abuse Services

Teaching a non-verbal autistic person to perform the simplest task is sometimes a waste of precious resources that could be used to a greater advantage in trying to educate the non-verbal autistic in academics.

The autistic person is usually viewed as retarded with a mental age far below his chronological age, with no hope of achieving physical independence and even less hope for achieving mental proficiency in any subject area. The non-verbal autistic person is placed in this light because the professional community placed him there. They did so based on the results of tests given to him that were designed, for the most part, to measure the capabilities of a person who can communicate through some means, including spoken or written language, sign language, or the use of a picture vocabulary system.

Each of these methods provides a means whereby an idea or a thought can be transferred from the mind of one person to the mind of another person. When this possibility exists, then there exists the possibility for communication to take place. Without communication, there exists no way to verify the accumulated sensory information with a reliable source who is watching out for him, and as a result, the non-verbal as he has retained valid information. If ideas are formed on the basis of this erroneous mix of real and unreal, truths and untruths, formed from this mix in the mind of each non-verbal non-communicative person then, for these people to face reality on your terms with your understanding of it, remains an impossibility.

Each question that requires an absolute single word answer, like many of the tests that are given to the non-verbal, non-communicative person by any number of professionals, would tell you nothing about the non-verbal, non-communicative person's real mental abilities or his mental capacity. The unfortunate aspect of this sampling and testing is that what you normally receive as a one word answer to your test questions rarely tells what we non-verbal autistics are thinking, as a longer and more complex idea often forms in our minds that contains the single word answer that is needed to answer your question. In this situation, retrieving the one word often is impossible but retrieving the entire thought that contains the one word answer is much easier for the non-verbal autistic person to do.

Finding the one word that is needed is like finding the needle in the haystack. It is usually easier to find the haystack than it is to find the needle.

The point that I want each of you people, who are here as a faculty member of a day-program, a residential program or who are involved in the care of a non-verbal autistic individual, to remember is to resist the pitfall that has been created for you by the testing that was done by the professional community. They take the results as the word of God and, as such, are never ever to be questioned or even doubted by a person of a lesser socio-economic position than themselves, meaning you. Resist tripping over the pitfall that we non-verbal autistic people do not have the mental capacity to think rationally, nor to develop a personality, nor to comprehend the information that we are exposed to each time that we encounter reality, nor react to stimuli, either physical or mental, that is age appropriate. To rethink what each non-verbal autistic person is capable of doing is to end the way that people envision us as worthless and is to add value to our being as truly intelligent though lacking the ability to speak. In this light, we are all equal to each other in many ways that are not considered at this time to be a possibility.

Important enough is what you think the non-verbal autistic person's capabilities are as a result of your being here today. The way we are now perceived by you tests your desire to rethink your ideas and thoughts about us and to raise questions about the placement and the programs that have been developed for us. Each of the non-verbal autistic people who are presenting at this session can testify that education helped them to progress to where they are at present as far as their abilities to not only face you in this meeting, but to face our realities daily, regardless of our handicaps.

I've previously answered people's questions about what helped me to achieve the level of understanding that I am in possession of. I can't imagine telling these people anything other than what I've said in the past. I tell them, as I am telling you now, that you must help us fulfill our need to be included in your world as a contributing member of society without being just a freeloader.

Too often, *education* means going to school as most if not all of you have done. Yet, when I use the term *education*, I am using it in a broader sense that could include formal schooling as well as anything else that would act as a vector in bringing to our minds any type of truthful information that will link us to reality and to your world. Educational radio and educational TV, world news and commentary, being read to or listening to books on tape, watching educational videos on any number of subjects, simply being talked to about what is taking place around us are some of the vectors that are very successful in supplying us with useful information as well as linking us to your world and to you.

Testing us with the methods that essentially are involved in testing a person who is capable of communicating in some way is not an appropriate means for determining the mental ability relative to the non-verbal autistic person. You must develop a trusting relationship with the non-verbal autistic person to determine for yourself what his abilities and capabilities are. Teaching the non-verbal autistic person to retie his shoes is not as important to his understanding the world around him as is your telling him, in terms that are age-appropriate, the highlights of recent or future events that will have an effect on his life.

Earlier, I said that it is more important to educate the non-verbal autistic person rather than to waste precious resources in trying to teach him a simple task, like fitting yellow round pegs into round holes or taking flashlights apart and reassembling them. I stand firm on this issue unless the student understands the importance of this task and understands the relevance that learning it will have on his life. Remember, please, that we have minds that need to be both stimulated and challenged by being educated.

Thank you for your attention and for coming to this session.

About the Author

Wallace (Wally) Wojitowicz, Jr. was born 12/18/66 and is now 36 years old. He lives in the Clifton Park area of upstate New York with his parents, Wallace and Gayalyn Wojitowicz. Wally has lived at home all of his life. Wally has two sisters—Jane, who is a year-and-a-half older than he, and Jennifer, who is two years younger. Wally has seven nieces and nephews, two grandmothers, and many aunts, uncles, and cousins. Wally enjoys all of his family.

Wally was diagnosed as autistic at age two. He developed epilepsy at age nine and has grand mal seizures. Wally has some slight involvement with Tourette's Syndrome, cerebral palsy, and obsessive-compulsive disorder.

During February of 1992, at the age of 25, Wally was introduced to facilitated communication (FC) because he is non-verbal. Since that time, FC has been his primary means of communication. Wally uses FC to communicate with his family and friends and to write. Through his writing Wally has been able to assist college students with course work and with term papers they have written on autism or on the autistic person. Some of Wally's work has been presented at autism conferences, published in newsletters, and published in books and articles about autism.

Wally attended various day programs that were available in his area from the time he was three until 1998. During 1998, Wally told his parents that he did not want to continue with the day program because there was nothing there for him to stimulate his mind. At Wally's urging, a decision was made by his parents that allowed him to stay at home and work on his writing. Wally was able to participate in two college level courses, one in Human Services and the other in basic Chemistry. Wally was scheduled to take a Sociology course

163

at a local community college, but because of his deteriorating health, he was not able to attend the course. He did, however, do all of the required reading for the course. At the present time Wally is still able to write using FC and a laptop computer. In 1997-98 Wally was able to type with both his left and right index fingers simultaneously on two computers. By utilizing the two computers he was able to carry on two separate conversations with two facilitators simultaneously, and at times one conversation would be in English and the other in French.

Since 1998 Wally has slowly lost the use of his left hand and arm and of all but the index finger on his right hand. He now has the use of just his right index finger. These losses are a result of the slow neuromuscular deterioration caused by ALS, a neurodegenerative disease. Wally was diagnosed with ALS in September of 2002.

At this point in time it is not known how long he will maintain control of his right index finger and be able to use FC. Now Wally writes almost every day for one to two hours. Previous to the onset of ALS, Wally was able to write up to five hours each day. At present a portion of his time is taken up with physical and occupational therapy which are necessary because of ALS and his deteriorating physical condition. In addition to writing, Wally enjoys reading, listening to classical music and books on tape, talk radio, traveling, and going for rides.

Two years ago, using FC, Wally told his parents that he wanted to speak the words that he writes. As a result of this request Wally has been receiving speech therapy and is now able to ask and answer questions with single words or short phrases. Wally still relies on FC for his formal communications and for longer conversations with friends and family.

Wally can be reached at wallyw1@juno.com

Chandima (Chammi) Rajapatirana

I Have Words Now

Tash 2002, Boston

The day my mother put me at my brother's computer and asked me to type my name was my true birthday. I lived in an abyss till then.

Greatest day of my life was that day. I hoped that the fear was over.

Accustomed to living in the abyss, coming up to the light was hard. Beset by memories, I am still terrified. Terrified that I might go back there. If FC were taken away from me, that is where I would be.

Assisting my great ascent was mom's task. I was filled with rage. Rage that I had spent eighteen years in a silent abyss. I raged at God for abandoning me. Asserting my rage was very important that first year. Because of my anger, my mom took me to a psychiatrist. Aware I need to live calmly, I go to therapy still.

Eased by being able to express myself, I feel better. Yet inordinately great rage takes me over sometimes. Dear mom has to remind me I have words now. Yes, I do forget that often. Finding my voice made life utterly wonderful; yet, greatly freeing my voice brought its own difficulties, too.

I urged my mom to get me into a real school; little realizing the homework I would get would almost outrun my desire to get friends. Bitterly, I realized some of my teachers did not accept me as an intelligent person. Trying to stay in Mr. Douglas' English class was hardest. Beset by his rude comments, I left his class. I loved history, earth science, and math. I had great teachers and made friends with peers. It is ironic that my English teachers had such difficulty accepting me. Perhaps they considered my writing too good to be truly mine.

I love writing and talking to dear friends. Realizing life-long dream of bantering with friends is possible because of FC. Hellish to sit by while other people talk and laugh. Yes, I remember that time well. I am not there now, yet I remember well the rage. The anguish I felt comes back and I am lost. . . until I remember I have words now.

FC freed my voice. I am now able to order my life through typing. I listen to lilting country music songs, hoping I sing some day. Typing has led to speech for several FC users. I am working on this myself. Quite soon I hope you will hear me effortlessly delivering the speeches I have typed. That would be the best gift of all.

Uplifting to think of all the gifts FC has brought me. There is something I have never talked about in public. I am wetting my lips in trepidation. Immutable, vise-like grip of depression was also eased after FC. In fact, until I got FC I had hoped to die. I refused repetitive attempts to teach me to swallow pills. I had no means to tell mom when I had a headache. Times when she guessed correctly that I had a headache, I still didn't take the Tylenol she would try to give. I just tried to kill myself by not swallowing pills. Doing FC finally gave me a reason to live. Yes, the first time I was able to tell mom I had a headache, dear mom offered me two Tylenols; I swallowed them without any problem. I simply quit being stubborn. Trying to kill myself without medicine, I likely endured a lot of pain.

Not the least of the pain I endured was the work I was taught. Until FC I was destined to be cleaning floors. Of course the people who tried to teach me such skills had a hellish time.

FC made people say, "Yes, he is intelligent."

I love the books mom brings me now. I love my tutors. I love exercising my brain. I am a burgeoning writer now. Think of that.

Brightening my life is the greatest gift FC brings me. Lilting life today is possible, thanks to FC. College is still a dream. I just got FC too late in life to make realizing this dream easy. I lived for so long in my silent abyss that my rage is so near the surface. I feel enraged to see other students working so easily. Returning to try college will mean I have to conquer envy. I hope to try college soon.

Meditating on my life before and after FC has done me a world of good. I lost my impatience regarding the things still missing in my life. Wearying to live consumed by rage. I hope, I believe, I know that nothing is beyond my reach now that I have words.

About the Author

I lived in Sri Lanka until I was eighteen months old. My family and I moved to the US at that time. I lived in a silent abyss until I was almost eighteen years old. I endured years of yearning, countless hours of desolation, until facilitated communication rescued me. I was inert only outwardly;

now at last I could share my inner thoughts with others. I published a book of poems. My essays have been published in fine magazines, too. I am invited to present at conferences. Initially I needed a very tight hold on my hand to type. I can now type with a light touch on my shoulder. Altering my life, facilitated communication, together with a stubborn mom, gave me a reason to live.

I was delighted that AutCom elected me to be on their board. Social justice to all people is resting on the advocacy of organizations like AutCom and I am honored to be part of that.

Chandima can be reached at chammi@aol.com

Mike converses with his facilitator Carol on his Liberator

Mike Hoover

To Be a Good Helper

Presentation to TC's Community staff, a local micro board, in 1996

I think I need you to know some things about autism. I need you to know that the helpers who work with autistic people need to be patient and they need to understand that it is not possible to do things right away. I need you to understand that starting a thing is hard. The idea how to get it done does not connect with the action happening right away. The best way to deal with this is to wait patiently, or else help by showing the first step by doing it yourself, like taking an object and doing the same action.

The thing that is the most important to remember is that people with autism can understand a lot of things and do not like having other people talk about them as if they were not there in the room. The best way is to have the conversation in front of the person directed to them.

I need you to know that I need the helpers who work with me to have the idea that I am a capable person, and that they do not do things for me but do things *with* me. I need to have the helpers who work with me have the ability to hear my needs and hear my high interest in being independent. I need the helpers who work with me to be the kind of people who are my best friends and my best advocates, too. I need for my helpers to come to my house ready to be with me, not to do other things in my house, but to have fun with me or work together with me. I think the helpers who come in my house have the right to have their own time for phoning home and things like that.

I hope you have had a good meeting and I hope you have the best ideas to share with each other. I need you to know that the reason people with autism are angry a lot is because they feel different from others. Sounds and the things around them have a different effect than the way others feel them. Reasons for this I do not know. I know the only thing that is really hard for me is having a bad bedtime and not sleeping well. I have sleep apnea.

I think the autism is stronger in some people. I need the helpers to hear how others with autism feel by reading books by Temple Grandin and Thomas McKean and Donna Williams.

Have the best time of your life working together to help others have a life full of joy and opportunity. Another thing is to remember the idea that people with autism are the best of us all because they have to work so hard just to have a chance to be in the community.

I had a hard time doing this. I need others to get a better understanding of autism. I need the helpers here to know the best things they are doing are okay. I need the helpers to be as patient as they can be and not have a hard time just waiting for things to be different. The main thing for me is being with someone to help me be safe and do the things that I want to do.

Mike Hoover

Mike Hoover of Boulder, Colorado has been invited to give presentations several times at a large church in Loveland, Colorado. This presentation to teachers and church leaders several years ago was about people who use communication devices.

Using Communication Devices In Church

The thing I need you to know about helping the people in your church who use assistive technology is that it is important for the teacher to wait while they find the words they want to say. Just because people do not use their voice does not mean they are stupid or that they have nothing to tell you. The biggest challenge for me is when I need something and have trouble communicating it to others. I need you to know how important it is to find out how a person communicates and how they need to be helped in order to participate in church. I need you to know how important it is for the people who use assistive devices to have a chance to be included in talks and in giving testimony the same as everyone.

I need you to know about this machine. It is called a Liberator. I use it every day to talk to friends and family and to help give talks like this one. I have learned a language called Minspeak that I use for every day conversations, but when writing things like talks and letters, I use facilitated communication (FC). I began using FC in 1992. I used it in school, at home, and with my friends. I need you to understand that when I have someone support my hand, I choose the words. You need to help people who use FC to have more trained partners who help them in their typing. The thing that is hard is being consistent and typing every day. Another thing is that the helpers need to be sure they are supporting the person, not guiding them.

I need you to know I have a testimony of Jesus Christ. I need you to understand how he has given this blessing to people who cannot use their voice. My belief in Jesus Christ has been the thing that helped to keep me from going crazy when I could not tell people how I felt or the things I needed.

171

Mike Hoover

I need you to help all who need FC to have access to it. That's all for now. Amen.

About the Author

Mike Hoover, 31, lives in Boulder, Colorado. He is a strong advocate for people with disabilities. He has given public presentations and trainings throughout Colorado and in other states. He started using Facilitated Communication in 1992 with friends from Boulder Parks and Recreation who attended a Doug Biklen training in Denver. Mike graduated from Fairview High School in 1993. He works at Books West, a book distribution company where he is valued for his enthusiasm and hard work.

Mike loves trains, music, getting a massage, volunteering in the community, and being with friends. He has been on the Colorado TASH board and is a member of Watch Our Words, an FC users group.

You can contact Mike at dldown@qwest.net

Dan Treacy

Facts for Caregivers 101

Presented at the 11th Annual Direct Service Conference
sponsored by the Maine Department of Mental Health,
Mental Retardation & Substance Abuse Services,
Bangor, Maine, 1998

Did you think when you started to work with disabled people
that you would come across someone like me? Well, there are
lots of "someones" like me. I may be unable to dress myself
completely, or make myself a sandwich or bathe myself. I may
be unable even to turn the pages in a book.

This is what autism is like. Many people with autism
have no speech or speech that is undecipherable to others.
Often speech consists of echoes, repeating words or phrases
recently heard but which have no bearing on the current
conversation. Sometimes we make sounds that to you may
sound like moaning, or to put it more pleasantly, like humming.
We are only releasing speech energy which has no other
outlet. Occasionally, I am able to make a sound which to me

sounds like real melodic humming. I love the music I make in my mind.

Serious miscues are happening in our brains that affect the proper operation of our bodies just as a defective electrical cord might affect the operation of a lamp or a radio. Bad seizures can result from the interruption in current in the brain. Mini-seizures like I have can create big problems, too. Sometimes behavior that is alarming or simply annoying is a release of energy and is usually out of the control of the person with autism.

Some of us with autism are also afflicted with another overpowering disability called obsessive compulsive disorder; some call it OCD. Call it whatever you like, it's a bitch to live with.

While I write this morning, my body is in a terrible OCD frenzy. I have taken Zyprexa, but it takes a long time to work. Medicine helps me somewhat, and they have me on a gluten-free, caseine-free diet, and that helps a lot. I don't always have this symptom, but when I do, it is really incredible. To anyone watching, I suppose it looks like the behavior of a retarded person. OCD is hard for me to bear because of the shame I feel about causing those I love such frustration and extra work.

Obsessive behavior is something that the person cannot control by himself. In my case, sometimes a ride in the car or a long walk will help with the OCD. Objects that are handled compulsively and might be damaged should be hidden, but you should always substitute a more appropriate item. It gives me sensory delight to absorb the feel of, for example, a sock or a cake of soap or a dismembered fountain pen. I call it feeding my skin.

Those outside my immediate family don't understand at all. Sometimes my family doesn't understand, either. Even I don't understand why it happens to me. Who could explain this behavior from a thirty-one year old man?

Witnessing this kind of racing, tapping, useless expenditure of energy must be shocking at first. Then, as schedules and plans are affected, frustration begins, then annoyance. When you don't understand the cause of this behavior, anger, quite naturally, rears its head, and tempers are lost. Degrading remarks are sometimes made, and even violence can become a factor.

You must try not to get frustrated by this inappropriate behavior because angry people sometimes say cruel things which we can understand. Remember, too, we can sense ridicule and rejection in people's stares. We don't want to cause disruption. It's beyond our control.

Above all things, if I don't get any other part of my message across, remember that we understand your every word and gesture. Never forget that.

What we are often unable to do is command obedience from our bodies. We can't make our bodies follow our own brain's directions, so don't always expect obedience to your requests. Especially immediate obedience. No doubt you have seen a person with autism perseverate or get stuck while performing a task. Maybe he seems not to hear you. Maybe he is wearing a pleasant expression and seems to be deliberately defying you or teasing you. Give him a break and realize his brain has to sort out the commands. Maybe if he can't follow your requests fully, he might be able to compensate and do it his way, the way his brain's message directs him.

Also, always think of the autistic person with respect, remembering that this person is somebody's son or daughter, sister or brother, maybe lost from parental love because of a fearful disability and probably completely misunderstood. Parents are told by professionals to institutionalize their children with autism when it is really preferable to arrange to provide care to support them at home. I think it makes better fiscal sense and it is more humane to help families stay together. I realize that parents age and fall ill, but by that time a back-up plan should be in place. Herding disabled people around like so many cattle is a sure way to reduce the dignity of each of those souls. Dreary thoughts of my own long-term situation assail my mind, but making changes or plans for my future is out of my hands at this time.

Performing the simplest bodily care is what I need help with. I like to be fresh and clean just like anyone else. My nose runs like anyone else's, and I need help to wipe it. I need help to wipe my butt.

Some of this stuff is very much like the care you would bestow on an infant, yet I can't provide it for myself at any time. Someone must cut my meat and wipe my face after a meal, just like a child. My apraxia prevents me from doing the simplest routine self-care. It is not stubbornness, a lack of discipline, nor a psychological hangup. I can't make my body do the things I want to do. I'm like a puppet, controlled by a power outside his own body, but craving the opportunity to live like all of you.

Each person with autism is different and has individual needs to be met. We can't speak in words of our needs, but remember that silence does not mean our needs don't exist or make them less urgent. I am relying on people like you to create an opportunity for me to accomplish with dignity all I am able to accomplish and to free myself from the prison of isolation and fear awaiting me.

Finding a caregiver who understands my situation but respects me as a living, feeling, thinking, human being is what I dream of, someone like Annie Sullivan who assisted Helen Keller.

My friends Wally and Tom and others I have met with autism have brilliant minds. I believe that Wally is a true genius. Yet he and Tom and I are simply going to function and be regarded as retarded adults with some pretty weird behaviors unless we get support from dedicated people, especially people who have the qualities I listed. The big number one qualification is the ability to use facilitated communication (FC), and most of all, the interest to apply it.

When I was 25 years old, I was introduced to FC. My life finally started to have meaning. I am now able to express affection for my family and appreciation for those who help me. I never went to school at all, only to day treatment for the profoundly retarded. Did I ever shock them when they discovered that I could read and understand everything.

While FC is a wonderful way for me to communicate, the current outlook for FC is dismal in New York because people in authority don't look favorably on it.

I know many folks who use FC whose lives have been changed. I attend group therapy sessions in Connecticut with six young men and three young ladies who have autism and who use FC. Each person brings his own facilitator, and we have a ball.

Some people believe real communication requires a voice. I tell you that communication really comes from the heart. Our group discusses all topics that any group of young people might be interested in. We talk about our problems and share each other's pain.

Three of our group attend college. Michael is a published poet and Katie sings and plays the piano beautifully, yet she does not speak at all. We all feel a closeness and affection for each other, each of us really enriching the other. I am very fortunate to have found them, and I know I'm blessed by the association.

We are also blessed by our association with Curt Brown and Carleen. We met Curt at an FC conference in Syracuse a couple of years ago. Curt gathered materials written by people who use FC, combined it with some gorgeous photography, and created a marvelous videotape.

Some of the readings were done by children and some by Curt himself. It was done with great affection, and I think it is a masterpiece.

It was through Curt that we were offered the opportunity to be here today. I hope I have said something to help you understand about my kind of autism.

Curt said that there was to be a question period after the presentation. Please don't think that any questions about autism will upset me or hurt my feelings. It was a privilege for me to share this with you today. Thank you all.

Dan Treacy

About the Author

My life story so far is rather dull. I was born on November 19, 1966, the youngest child in a family of five sisters and two brothers. My development was far from normal. I was lacking in speech, coordination and body control. But I was always, always smart, and no one knew it at all. I was in day treatment programs all my life.

No schooling was what I received as it turned out. I did get lots of mileage on the school bus but not much else to challenge my unstimulated mind. My behaviour was decidedly bizarre, so except for occasional family functions, I didn't get to go many places.

From the day facilitated communication was introduced to me in February, 1992, I knew my life would change. Yet it has been a frustrating, sometimes agonizing struggle against my own seriously bedeviled body as well as against the ignorance and fear of family and even some professionals I have known.

I am an Association for Retarded Citizens dropout. I couldn't bear to spend my days with no hope for an interesting activity or a conversation to eavesdrop on or participate in.

I live at home with my mother in a little town near West Point, New York. I spend lots of time on the computer or listening to books or music on tape. I also spend about ten hours per week with a very understanding man named Matt Sullivan who facilitates with me. Matt takes me walking or to the mall and to see women's baseball games at West Point in the spring.

Mother recently found a new gastroenterologist who has had great success in treating my chronic severe gastric pain. As a result of his treatment, my obsessive compulsive disorder has also improved greatly.

I am a very big man. My size intimidates many people

which causes additional obstacles to my ambitions for an independent life. Each challenge is there for me to complain about, to fear, or to face. My hope is that I may have the courage to keep on trying.

I hope you enjoy my writings as much as I enjoy composing them. Feel free to share questions or comments with Dan at:

Dan Treacy at Dansaltpoint@aol.com

Ian, enjoying the sun in Charleston Harbor

Ian Wetherbee

Realities of Autism

This paper was originally presented at the Illinois TASH Conference on February 22, 1999, in Chicago

Below are excerpts from columns that I have written for my college newspaper. Sometimes I use my column to let my fellow students catch a glimpse of who I am inside this autistic body. Most of the time they act kind of scared of me. Maybe the following quote from the book *Skallagrig* by William Horwood explains this fear. It was made about a girl named Esther with cerebral palsy.

He knew it was not that people were cruel or malevolent, it was simply that they could not cope with the affront Esther made to normality. To believe that such a being could think was barely thinkable. For to do so was to imagine what it must be like to be her...

...so I try to let them know that I'm human and that I'm more than just someone who is able to pass my classes and

181

study in the library.

Here I try to communicate that my body usually isn't in my own control.

Most people's time rests in their own control. You may think that other people have control of your life and that you are not free to choose your own way. You may think that parents and professors and officers of the law and deans and marriage partners and fiancées and roommates and employers make your decisions for you. You may think you are captive to your own desire for fun, power or popularity. This is not so.

All of these people and your own inner nature do try to influence your actions. Sometimes they enforce rules on you. They offer consequences for your actions. Sometimes these influences are good and sometimes they are bad. Sometimes they hold open doors to whole new worlds and sometimes they try to slam doors shut on other possible futures. But you and only you choose exactly how you act.

Some people don't have even that choice. I am one of those people, almost. As far back as I can remember, I couldn't do much of what I wanted to do. First of all, I can't talk. Right on the tip of my tongue would be what I'd want to say, but I could only think it, not say it. You may have sometime said something, only to wish you could take it back --- not me. Maybe you made someone happy by saying you love him or her --- not me. I can only know inside my head what I would have said.

I couldn't often make my body do things that I'd like it to do. I can't write with a pencil or pen. I can't easily hug someone. I lose control when I'm too excited or upset. That is why I often try to run away just when a movie is getting good or when I am about to win a game or lose a game.

People judged how smart I was by my actions. Because I couldn't choose to do physically those actions that I wanted to do, everyone thought that I was mentally handicapped. When the time came to go to school, I went to special education classes. I couldn't do most of the things they wanted me to do in school and I still can't do most of them, because they require more body control than I have. They were things like matching colors by picking up a card and putting it on another card of the same color or putting puzzles together. My teachers thought I didn't know my colors and shapes, but actually I couldn't put things where I wanted to when I wanted to. I did choose to try because everyone cared about me so much and didn't understand why I couldn't do those silly tasks.

I wasn't able to not do my homework because I never had any homework. I also wasn't able to cheat on tests because I never took any tests. All that I learned about math and reading came from listening to TV and listening to teachers teach other kids. No courses in history or English were offered to me to survey and choose between. I didn't choose to go to special ed. classes either. I didn't choose anything except to try my best.

God then did a miracle in my life. He showed my dad and mom and teachers a way for me to communicate using something called facilitated communication or FC. Suddenly I could go to school in regular classes with normal kids. Finally someone showed me how to do math right and explained history to me. Always, I still need an adult to go everywhere with me to help me communicate and to help me with the things I can't do myself, which is about everything.

Guess what? I still can't not do my homework or cheat on a test, but now it's because I have that adult there every second, watching my every move. Guess what else? I hardly ever mind. Learning to me is like a long drink of water after a long time spent in a dry wasteland.

Other choices have finally been given to me. I can order in a restaurant. I can tell my family that I love them. I can make Purdue jokes and cheer for IU. I can play games.

You make choices everyday that shape your lives. Sometimes you may wish you were like me and not have to choose. Most of the time you probably take those choices for granted. Cherish them and make wise decisions.

In another column I wrote about how life was for me before anyone knew that I didn't have mental retardation. I try to show that life can be good even for those who are or who are thought to be mentally disabled.

I really believe that disabled persons enjoy life as much as persons who aren't handicapped do. I am autistic and, until I was thirteen years old, people thought that I was very mentally disabled. I am unable to talk and couldn't tell anyone that I'm not mentally handicapped. They couldn't know that I liked my life and had chosen to live each day as a gift from God.

They also couldn't know that I was able to follow and enjoy intellectually challenging conversations, television shows, movies and dissertations. I believe that many other people thought to be mentally disabled are as I am; not mentally impaired at all, although their physical appearance might suggest otherwise. They are quite seriously handicapped but are mentally sound. I believe that they, too, can intellectually understand our world and that they, like me, enjoy living and live each day having happiness and sadness and love and joy.

I have good friends who love me now and who loved me even when they thought I was retarded. Being loved unconditionally makes life worth living. No degree of impairment that they saw in me kept them from loving me. My feelings of self worth grew from their acceptance of me.

I believe that even if a person is mentally handicapped, their life can be good. I spent years in a severely mentally and physically handicapped classroom and also spent time in a moderately mentally handicapped classroom. Many of my friends and classmates were mentally handicapped. They had a wonderful time each day in school. Each one entered into life needing extra care and depended on others for even the simplest things. They know how to love unconditionally and I never forget their friendship. Not only do they like living; they make others' lives brighter for having known them.

This next paragraph was my first attempt in my column to set people at their ease when they see me. I didn't want them to judge who I am just by my appearance.

Of course, no one can visit Huntington College without walking through the campus grounds. The landscaped lawns and walks always impress me whenever I'm between buildings, but more impressive yet to me are the friendly people I pass as I'm making my journeys along those walks. I know how strange I look as I walk along on my tiptoes, not often seeming to look at passers by. Despite my appearance, many that pass me make sure to say, "Hi, Ian." Hear me now. Regardless of how I look, I hear you and just wish I could answer back. I love all of you.

I went to a play called *The Diviners* at which I got so into the plot that my dad practically had to sit on me to keep me from running right up on the stage. I reviewed the play in my column. At the start of that column, this is how I tried to let those who saw me that night know why I was so wild and to know how difficult it is for me to stay in control.

Sometimes I am just not able to contain my actions and myself. Ninety percent of an autistic person's efforts while in public are spent trying to avoid inappropriate behaviors that "normal" people seem to be able to easily suppress. One place where I had a terrible time trying to sit still and not make noise was in the small theater watching the play "The Diviners."

I didn't have a terrible time at the play; quite the contrary. In fact, I loved this play. Deep into the drama, I relaxed my guard and was soon a noisy, rocking back and forth in my seat spectator. Good things don't often cause this reaction, so we might say that the Ian Wetherbee behavior-o-meter registered a four star reading for "The Diviners" and its excellent cast.

A main character of *The Diviners* was thought to be mentally retarded. I tried to let my readers see how perception affects how people treat other people, even when they have the best of intentions. Buddy is the retarded character in the play, who I thought was a lot smarter than he appeared...

From the time of his near drowning, Buddy wouldn't touch bath water because he thought water kept him from breathing. Sometimes all of us have fears that we don't completely conquer in our lives. We let them affect our decisions and our actions. Buddy needed help with his fear of water. Instead, Buddy was allowed to be dirty and infected with ringworm. Probably this failure to help Buddy further reflected people's view of his ability to understand and learn. They wouldn't have let anyone else live like that, but they must have felt that there was no way that Buddy would ever understand that his fear was irrational or that water could help him.

The next column is meant to show that I have a sense of humor and that even though I'm smart, I still do autistic things. Maybe it will help someone in the future to know enough to not use the stall for the handicapped.

December is a tough month to travel in. This isn't because of icy road conditions or deep snowdrifts. It's because of the heavy coat I have to wear. Only someone who needs assistance in the restroom can fully appreciate why that is.

Without getting specific, I need some help when I go to the bathroom. Somebody, sometimes my brother Todd, but usually my dad, has to be with me during the whole operation. Between my dad and I, we probably weigh 500 pounds and stand thirteen feet high. We need lots of room!

Thanks be to God for the stalls for the handicapped found in most public bathrooms today in America, which have room for both my helper and me. Let me tell you of our five hundred pound adventures, experienced in bathrooms everywhere.

Under the door of a toilet stall can usually be seen one pair of feet. In my stall are seen four feet. Heads are normally only seen briefly above a stall's walls. My helper's head is always seen above my stall's walls while waiting to assist me and my head joins the view at the start and end of each visit. I sometimes make strange noises, not by design but by accident, due to my autism. These out of the ordinary restroom sights and sounds catch people's attention.

One such time was on the campus of Anderson University. We were attending the Anderson Church of God state youth convention. This time we were in the handicapped stall of a very busy restroom in Reardon Auditorium. I yelled out a strange noise as I often do. Soon, a security man was knocking on the door of our stall, demanding to know what was happening in there. We came out and Dad tried to explain. The more he said, the more skeptical the security man grew, the more interested the people around us turned, the more red Dad's face became and the more autistic I acted. In the end our accuser retreated in confusion, and later, realizing his mistake, came and visited me for a chat.

Funny now, but not funny then, are some of the experiences we have had because someone else was already using the handicapped stall. Squeezing both of us into one normal sized stall is next to impossible. Men's rooms are usually crowded at highway rest stops, providing lots of curious eyes when unusual things happen. My antics can often catch people's attention.

Once, the door to our too small stall had a broken latch. Every time Dad tried to help me, his derriere would bump the door and it would pop open, leaving me open to everyone's perusal. Dad would yank the door shut, but it would soon happen again. By the time I was done, it seemed like half of the guys in the rest room had a view of the inside of my stall.

Even when I am done and out of the stall, I can be a source of entertainment. Any hot air hand dryer is irresistible to me. I'll hit the button and enjoy the hot air on my hands. If I can, I'll turn on every dryer in the room at once, so I can also enjoy their combined noise. If Dad doesn't watch me closely enough and the row of urinals are parallel to the stalls and close to them also, I may dash along the row of urinals, nudging each user into the urinal as I pass. As Dad apologizes to the angry and wet bathroom clients, they show little willingness to come around to the understanding that I didn't mean to bump them but was just running around.

Changing back from embarrassing moments to my first statement about winter clothes, even in a handicapped stall, two bundled up people don't fit very well. The choice is between leaving the coats in the car while dashing to the rest stop or not fitting in the stall. We usually choose the cold. If only I could also choose to always have an empty bathroom except for my helper and me, maybe I could avoid all of these other complications, too.

This is my back to school column. Having insecurities is common to everyone and being autistic may sometimes actually be helpful.

The best of times and the worst of times – that describes my summers. After a great but challenging first year of college, including a summer school course, I was really, utterly ready for a vacation. Happily, I just sort of crashed at home for a few days. Then the boredom set in.

Understand me, I love being with my family. However, too much of a good thing isn't always so great. Doing little outside the house except shopping at Wal-Mart and lifting weights at the MPEC leaves me dopey and not very alert. I needed a job, but I'm really unable to have a normal job, due to my autism. I cannot control my body to do physical labor, though I am quite strong. On my own, I can't do tasks that require good hand and eye coordination. I am smart, but I can't show my intelligence without a trained person to facilitate my communication.

Lots of people have hard lives and go on with life anyhow. Very few people choose their own handicaps, and few people are completely content with their lot in life. Know that I wish under every star in the sky that I could talk and that I wasn't autistic.

In high school, when I went to my chemistry lab, I sometimes would have one of my pity parties. I would keep thinking about my disability and how I needed two people to sit on either side of me so I wouldn't hurt myself on the experiments we were doing. "Why," I thought, "people must think I am an idiot or something."

The other students in the lab might not see past my outer appearance and therefore miss who I am. Girls will miss my very handsome face. The guys across the room seem to be laughing at me. My mind was racing away with my sanity, and I was falling deeper and deeper into my pit of despair.

These thoughts may remind you of a similar time in your life. When I first went to high school, these thoughts would lead to an out-of-control screaming fit that made everyone *around me duck for cover. My dad then explained that every high school student had those same thoughts. When I have them now, I remember that inside my autistic body, I am just like everybody else. We have the same insecurities and fears. No one escapes pity parties.*

This reminder to myself actually cheers me up. It also gives me insight into why other people act kind of weird sometimes. I have screaming fits, others try to impress people by boasting or by making fun of somebody else or by dressing on the edge of public decency. Some find friends with whom they don't feel insecure, and some just act aloof.

Wait, being unable to talk isn't so bad after all. Maybe a good scream isn't the worst thing that a pit of pity leads to.

Going bananas and embarrassing myself isn't really something I am proud of. I am most proud that I haven't had a screaming fit in a long time. I don't have any trouble seeing that my reaction to feelings of insecurity isn't good. For others, recognizing what their reaction is might not be so simple. Doing away with their silly behavior might not be an easy thing to do.

I guess all of our lives have both the best of times and the worst of times. Maybe my summer wasn't so terrible. One thing is for sure. I'm very glad to be back on the Huntington College campus again.

About the Author

My name is Ian Wetherbee, and I'm from Huntington, Indiana. I am 25 and have one brother, Todd, who is married and lives in Indianapolis. I'm a senior at Huntington College, where my dad is a math professor. I live at home with my mom and dad. I have a facilitator/personal assistant who goes with me to my college classes, and facilitated communication has been my link to the rest of the world since I was thirteen years old. Facilitated communication has freed me from the silence and isolation of the world of the "perceived to be retarded." One of my goals in life is to help everyone else who still remains in that isolation to join me in my freedom.

Feel free to share questions or comments with Ian at iwetherb@comcast.net

Jean-Paul with his wife Debbie

Jean-Paul Bovee

Employment and People on the Autism Spectrum

Jean-Paul has spoken on a variety of topics on autism throughout the United States. He expanded on this topic for our book as he speaks only from notes.

Employment is a hard area for those of us on the spectrum. As Cary Griffen of the University of Montana says on this subject, "95% of people with autism spectrum differences are unemployed or underemployed." This means that only 5% of people on the autism spectrum have jobs that pay decently or use their skills. It is an outrage and a disgrace to our "civilized" countries to waste this much talent. Even the programs that deal with people with developmental disabilities do not want to deal with people with autism spectrum differences, as we do not fit into their neat little categories. Such options here in the United States, like sheltered workshops or job training programs, have an easier time with people with Down Syndrome or Cerebral Palsy than with people on the Autism Spectrum. I have been very fortunate in that I was able to go to college and learn the bookwork to be able to be given chances to learn my job, but I have had my share of frustrating part-time jobs. The good thing was that my main job at the time was to be a student, and I was good at that. In fact, I will start mentioning my experiences and what helped me to succeed when so many others have not had my good fortune.

Prior to college, I did not hold any jobs. I grew up on a farm six miles outside of the town that I went to school in. The only work that I did, besides the usual chores and Saturday morning work on the farm, was to haul hay in the summer. It was hard work picking up square bales of hay and throwing them in the truck to take them to the barn and then throwing them up into the barn. I drove the truck quite often, too, even though I did not have my license. I only drove it in the fields. One did not make a lot of money at work like this, but I was happy with the money that I made. It was extra cash.

When I started college in 1986 at Southwest Missouri State University, Mom had a friend who was the head of the Microforms Department at the University Library. She gave me a chance at a job sorting papers and getting people microfilm and microfiche. After a semester, my job was switched to working in the Serials/Acquisitions Department, due to a faux pas that I made serving a university administrator. I treated him like any customer and did not defer or kow-tow to him in a sufficient manner, as far as he was concerned. The administrator wanted me fired. So my position was switched to another department to keep me on. I stayed in this position for the four years that I attended Southwest Missouri State University.

During the summer of my junior year at SMSU, I also held other part-time jobs to get extra money. My first non-library job was working as a dishwasher at a Mexican Villa restaurant. They had wanted an experienced dishwasher but gave me a chance. The job did not work out very well. Since I was inexperienced at dishwashing (at least commercially), I was switched to prep cook and that did not work well, either. They let me go after two weeks, saying to me that they liked my work ethic, but that they did not have the time or patience to have me learn as slowly as I was learning.

My second job of the summer was as a dishwasher at a Ryan's Family Steak House. That did not work out well, either. The management was really mean to the employees and they had 2/3 turnover every two weeks. It is amazing that the restaurant is still in business in Springfield. I could only tolerate being treated like crap for so long and put in my notice after four weeks. I could not stand working there any more.

When I started graduate school at the University of Kansas in 1990, I soon got a part-time job that lasted for one week. I applied to drive a mail van for the Continuing Education Department of the University. The van was very big and I could not see the side mirrors. The Friday of that week, I ran into a parked car. My employers and I parted ways. My class schedule changed, so this job was not going to work out anyway.

After a time of looking for another part-time job, I found a job in the Acquisitions Department of Watson Library, the University of Kansas main library. I worked there for over a year. My main focus was sorting and checking in gift books to the library system. I learned the other roles of acquisitions as well, but messed up in many areas as I did not ask questions when I did not understand things. After a year of messing up in certain areas, budget cuts sped up my departure. The only good thing about the timing was that I was about to take my written and oral compositions for my Master's Degree, and this gave me time to focus on the tests.

When I moved to Columbia, Missouri, during the summer of 1992 to get ready to start the Library and Informational Science program at the University of Missouri-Columbia, I worked several part-time jobs during my time in Columbia. I first got a job as a telemarketer. This lasted for about a week. My job was to sell cards that could be used to get meals in restaurants. These cards cost 68 dollars to purchase. This job did not work out for me, because I am not good at talking people into buying what they do not want and to not take no for an answer. After a week, my supervisor gave me a choice of working on suspension, which meant that I worked for no pay, or leave. Since I would not be paid for my work and I did not like it anyway, I left.

After a month of looking for a job, I found a job at Montgomery Ward in Home Furnishings. At that time, they had to give you a 90 day work evaluation on the job, so I was there for three months. After that time, the managers let me go. I was a good and efficient employee, always on time and ready to work. Looking back now, I see what lost me the job. First, I did not do small talk with the other employees and my supervisors. That is such a key thing. I have found that at work, only 20% of the time is spent doing the work. The other 80% of time is at the coffee machine, in offices, etcetera, talking and chatting with people. We who are on the spectrum are good at the first and not very good at the second. That is what hurts us. I also was not skilled at selling warranties when people did not want to buy them. I was not supposed to take no for an answer.

On none of the previous jobs did I mention that I was a person on the autism spectrum. I had a strong desire to make the job work on my own merits and not be treated like a second-class citizen. I am a very proud person and will not be treated with any less respect and dignity than any other person. However, not mentioning that I was a person on the autism spectrum was costing me employment. I was not being given the chances that maybe I could have had if I had been open about being on the autism spectrum. However, that is me.

I know of other people who have revealed being on the autism spectrum who have been penalized by losing their job. It is definitely a personal decision to disclose or not to disclose.

After a month, I got another job working as a bagger at a Price Chopper grocery store. Once I had been working there a week, I scheduled a meeting with the store manager. I mentioned to him that I was a person on the autism spectrum, and he asked me what modifications did I need to do my job. I think that he was thinking about physical modifications, but I told him that I needed extra time to learn my job to get it down. He responded, "Time—we have plenty of that!!" I worked there for nine months until I got an opportunity that I could not pass up. During that time, I worked with some very nice people and was one of the store's best baggers. I would also carry out groceries for elderly people who could not carry their own. In fact, one of my professors, his wife, and a ladyfriend of theirs were some of my best customers and would tip me for what I did. According to store rules, I was not supposed to accept tips, but I did anyway. I believe that if people tip you, they think that you are doing a great job and to not accept it would be to insult them and what they did. I think that the rule was to not solicit tips and I did not solicit tips. But, if people wanted to give them to me, I accepted.

In March of 1993, I spoke on a panel at the National Autism Symposium (Missouri's state autism conference). In the crowd that day were Jim Magruder, the Director of the Central Missouri Regional Center for Persons with Developmental Disabilities (CMRC), and Richard Strecker, the Regional Program Specialist for the Center. They heard me talk, and afterward, Richard talked with me about how I could fit into a position at CMRC. They had been thinking of having a disability/autism consultant, who was a person with a disability, to see how people in the region were being served and to give a personal take on these things. We kept in touch, and Richard got the paperwork done. I put in my two-weeks notice at Price Chopper at the end of August and started my new job at CMRC on September 7, 1993.

I stayed at this job until June of 1994. I was in my second year of my Master's program in Library and Informational Science. In this job, I got to travel with the case managers and training technicians to see the different programs, services, and residential areas in the central Missouri region to see how the people were being served. I was asked to be honest and tell Richard and Jim what I saw. Some places that we visited were very good to the people that they served and involved them in things that were important in their lives. Other places were the total opposite. I once visited a day program that had the people counting beans all day, because they had no work for them to do. Most of the people were in their 50's, 60's, and 70's, and the people running the place were in their 30's and 40's. The managers of the place called the workers our "boys" and "girls," which was insulting to me. These were people old enough to be my grandparents and they were treated like children because of their disabilities. To me, that was uncalled for, and I wrote up a report basically saying that. The operators of the day habilitation center were not happy with me and what I wrote, but that was my job. Things have improved since, and now the day habilitation program no longer exists. The people in the program live in group homes or individualized supported living and have been allowed to retire or get jobs in the community. So, things do change.

Another great opportunity that came out of this job was that Jim Magruder, our Director, was able to get me on committees within the Department of Mental Health, Division of Mental Retardation and Developmental Disabilities. I was on a committee called the Medicaid Waiver Steering Committee (now the Quality Framework Management Advisory Team—we have a new director who likes those kinds of terms). While I was on that committee, at the May, 1994, meeting, I met Kay Conklin, our state Developmental Disability Council Executive Director, who was also on the committee. I was finishing classwork for my Master's degree and was looking for employment. We were talking about that, and she pulled out a notice for a position as the Director of the Missouri

Developmental Disabilities Resource Center at the University of Missouri-Kansas City Institute for Human Development. I called and spoke to Vim Horn, the Associate Director of the Institute, who told me that it was the second week of interviews, but if I could overnight my cover letter and resume, he would take a look at it. So I skipped out on the afternoon of the meeting, went home, and got the cover letter and resume ready. I then went to the post office and overnighted the materials to the Institute. Vim got it on the following Monday and set up an interview for me two weeks later with himself, Kay Conklin, and Carl Calkins, the Director of the Institute. All three people knew that I was a person on the autism spectrum, so I did not have to explain that too much. They asked me questions to see if this was a job that I could do well. I answered the questions as well as I could, and they seemed to think that I would be good for the position, because I heard two weeks later that I had the job!! This was early June, and I was the first person in the Library and Informational Sciences class to get a job. The Institute wanted me to be able to start my job within two weeks, even though I stated that I could not go full-time until I had taken my written comprehensive exams, which were in July of 1994. I gave CMRC notice that I had gotten the job and that I was needed in Kansas City. On my last day, they threw a nice party for me and wished me well.

I started work as the Director of the Missouri Developmental Disabilities Resource Center in June of 1994, became full-time in July of 1994 and have been here ever since. My title has changed from director to manager to information specialist, and I have been doing most of the same things for the whole time. The last title fits me better than the other two, because it is more accurate to what I am doing. My main job is to answer requests for information and get people what they need. I am also in charge of maintaining and checking materials out from our library, including getting stuff back. I also do other projects for the Institute, such as being an advisor to the Kansas City, Missouri, Chapter of People First, a self-advocacy organization run by people with disabilities. I love the people that I work with and people seem to love how I do my job. Being on the autism spectrum has not been a detriment in my job, but a plus. From my own experiences, I can relate to families and people with disabilities. I know what people have been through, because I have been through a lot because of my differences.

That pretty well gives you the stories and personal examples. Now what I want to tell you are some of the things that are important to do and the lessons that I have learned from each. I learned most of my lessons the hard way, and as my Dad says, "When you learn the hard way, you learn!"

The first lesson is that when you need help, ask for it. Asking for help has been and is a hard thing for me. I am a proud man, and I hate doing things that might make me look stupid. But you will look stupid if you don't do things right because you have not asked for help. I still struggle with this area, but I am learning that you will not learn what you need to learn if you do not ask for help. My wife is getting onto me for that as well, so I am sure that this will be changing.

Second, make sure that you get to know your fellow co-workers and spend time talking with them. Truly, it is not how you do your job that keeps you there at work, it is how you get along with others that will make or break keeping a job. In my earlier jobs, I was not very interested in getting to know people. I was there to work and do my job. I did not understand that getting to know and work with people was more important on the job than dealing with the customer. I learned that through losing jobs. With the job at Price Chopper and later, this has not been a problem at all. I have always been a friendly person and I love to talk, so that is not an issue now. And I still get my other work done, too!!

Third, it helped me to disclose that I was a person on the autism spectrum. Others have been hurt by their disclosure of that fact. The Americans With Disabilities Act should protect people on the autism spectrum in the United States from being fired solely for being a person on the autism spectrum, but that is hard to prove and someone has to take your case. Disclosure is a personal decision, and each person has to determine whether it is best for him or her. For me, it was very helpful to do that, since my employers could understand me better and understand how I do things. I am different; that is a given. People on the autism spectrum are different in some ways from people who are not on the spectrum. But difference is what makes the world interesting and keeps the world going.

Finally, it helped me that my full-time job in school was my studies. I got financial aid, student loans, and help from the Missouri Divison of Vocational Rehabilitation, which tided me over during times in which I did not have extra money from jobs. I worked jobs that I knew I would not do forever so that I would have some extra money. The job that I hold now was my first full-time job since getting out of graduate school and I have been here over nine years. That is very good in an economy like this.

What are some of the options that people have once they are out of school and having to go into the work world or to college? Here are some of the options.

One option is to go into the military. Granted, most people on the autism spectrum will not see this as a logical choice or would not want to do this. However, the military does provide money for college in the future, and a person can learn skills that he or she could use later in life.

Second, a person could graduate and look for a job. That would take care of the employment situation and money very quickly. While jobs requiring only high-school diplomas are becoming more rare, not everyone is cut out for higher education.

Third, vocational schools and programs are a good way for many people to go. If the person is good with his or her hands, there are many skills such as auto work and building that people can learn at these schools and use to make a career.

Fourth, two-year or community colleges are a route to go as well. A person can learn a particular trade or take the lower-level classes and transfer to a four-year college or university. It is totally and completely up to them what they choose to do with their degree.

Finally, there are the four-year colleges and universities. This is the academic route and many of us have taken it. It has benefits and disadvantages. For those of us who do not have good hand skills and have to use our brains to survive, this is the way to go. Having my Masters' degrees is what got me this job. I knew that I would need an advanced degree to get a career, as I am not the most coordinated person in the world. However, this is not the route for everyone. Each person must know what they want to do and choose the route that will take them there.

Employment is something that we all need to do. Yet so few of us on the spectrum have good, meaningful work. There needs to be some help finding out what people want to do and fitting their talents to work. We cannot continue to waste such talents and skills. Our economy cannot handle that kind of waste.

About the Author

Jean-Paul Bovee is a 34 year old man on the autism spectrum. He has an M.A. in Medieval History from the University of Kansas, obtained in 1992, and an M.A. in Library and Informational Science from the University of Missouri-Columbia, obtained in 1994. Currently, he is an Information Specialist at the University of Missouri-Kansas City Institute for Human Development, Missouri Developmental Disabilities Resource Center.

Jean-Paul married the former Debbie Montgomery (she is Debbie Bovee now) on July 12, 2003, and is enjoying married life.

He has been speaking and writing on his experiences and on topics related to being on the spectrum for over seventeen years. He is an activist for improving our society's outlook towards people on the autism spectrum. Jean-Paul is interested in hearing from you.

Reach him at jpbovee7@hotmail.com

Kathy with her cat Vivir and some of her flags of the world

Kathy Grant

My Science Fiction World

Kathy originally presented part of this article at the Autism National Committee Conference in Arlington, Virginia in 1995. As a speaker she uses note cards for her presentations so didn't have a full write-up for us. She expanded this topic further in order for you to appreciate it fully.

Editors' note: *One of the myths of autism is that people within the spectrum do not have an imagination. This myth is based directly on the fact that the difficulties with communication do not allow those with autism to share their imaginations with us. However, the opposite is true. People within the spectrum have very active imaginations, and many use imaginary worlds as an escape from the overstimulation and boredom they experience in our world. These imaginary worlds are unique* to each individual and are complete with visual action of the most incredible detail. In this presentation, Kathy shares some of her imaginary world with us, a world which is closely connected to her interest in political science and the effects of discrimination.

In my science fiction of the 24th Century, I have created many different characters and planets. I will only touch on a couple of these things and how people with disabilities are treated in this unknown galaxy.

The main character of my science fiction is Keith Hill, an African-American man who is originally from the 20th Century, but who "arrived" in the 24th Century on the night the New York Yankees won the World Series against the Atlanta Braves in 1999. At the time of the 1999 World Series, Keith was living in Columbia, Missouri, working as a cashier at Kinko's. Keith is originally from St. Louis but decided to live in Columbia because several of his college friends were living there. In the 24th Century, Keith still lives in Columbia and started going back to school at the University of Missouri-Columbia (Mizzou), taking classes in post 20th Century history and philosophy.

In my science fiction, I have created aliens that are humanoids and aliens that are Numbers. The humanoid aliens I have created are the Rixyuians and the Cerephians. Rixyuians have a greenish-grey skin, small pointed ears, and purple or yellow eyes. All of them are bald and thin and have long life spans. Rixyu is a planet that has no countries, so nationalism is a hard concept for them to understand. Cerephians have bluish-grey skin and silver or white hair. They are stockier than Rixyuians, and their ears are not pointed. Like the Rixyuians, Cerephians have a hard time understanding nationalism.

Carillon and Sckgoggi are the planets inhabited by the Numbers. On both planets, the Numbers are 2 or 3 digits long, with the last digit being the sex organ. Odds are males and evens, excluding zero, are females. The reason why there are no zeroes in Carillonian or Sckoggian Numbers is that zero represents God.

Carillon has as many nations, tribes, languages, religions, and types of governments and economic systems as does Earth. The most powerful country on Carillon is Algebra, located on the continent of X3-27. Algebreans speak Numbre and border 2 countries, Geometry and Pythagoree.

In the 24th Century, Keith Hill learns that the Algebreans have a very dim view of their neighbors and actually consider Geometry to be an enemy, so much so that a demilitarized zone (DMZ) is set up all along the Algebrean–Geometran border, with chemical and biological weapons and troops. If Keith wants to take a trip to Geometry, he would have to go through Pythagoree to get there.

The planet Sckgoggi has only one continent but two racial groups, Whole Numbers and Fractions. Whole Numbers are usually the more wealthy, well educated, and politically powerful, whereas Fractions are the repressed minority in all areas of life. Vicious race wars plague Sckgoggi, leading many to emigrate to other planets, including Earth. Many who do emigrate to Earth come to the USA, hoping to rebuild their lives and hopes. Keith Hill's roommate, Acirema Oscinarf, is one who immigrated to the U.S. after seeing most of his family killed, hacked up by machetes and thrown into the Izeb River by Whole Numbers suspecting them of supporting Fractions in the struggle for equality, even though the Oscinarf family are Whole Numbers. One of the first things Keith noticed the 24th Century is that aliens from other planets and countries live, work, and go to school, and that all colleges and universities are part of the Galactic Economic Union (GEU). Keith Hill knows this and wonders why the Galactic Economic Union (GEU) doesn't do anything about straightening the political situation of any trouble spots in the known galaxy, and learned that the GEU only deals with economic, educational, scientific, transportation, and other matters not having to do with politics or diplomacy. The GEU's main function is to make sure that the known galaxy is doing well economically and educationally. Also, the GEU employs 12% of the adult population of the known galaxy. The GEU is headquartered on the planet Rronagia and has offices in every major planet, country, and city. Even Columbia has a GEU office, because Mizzou is part of the System of Colleges and Universities.

In the 24th Century, people with disabilities face much less discrimation and ignorance than they did in the 20th and early 21st Centuries. Keith finds it "amazing" that people with significant physical and developmental disabilities are in positions of power, are seen on TV, and play sports and have decent jobs along with the non-disabled population. He finds it refreshing to see that, for the most part, disabled people are seen as a natural part of life in the 24th Century, because back in the 20th Century, his only brother Cleo has autism and is non-verbal and living in a group home in St. Louis. There were so many times in the 20th Century that Keith wished that people saw Cleo as just a human being, especially at times when Cleo made funny noises or reacted differently in public because of his sensory issues.

Keith Hill is an African-American from the 20th Century who landed in the 24th Century by a lifetime fracture caused by the North Koreans who were secretly testing nuclear weapons. He came from a family of three siblings. His brother Cleo has autism and his sister Carolyn is neurotypical. His mother, Clara, was a teacher, and his father, Carl, was a factory worker in St. Louis.

In the 24th Century, Keith finds out that many disabled people have good jobs, live independently, hold positions of power (including political) and play very rough sports. He also finds out that augmentative communication devices are smaller than a dime, and many are smaller than a pin's head. Many of these nanite-sized devices, called FELICIAS, are put into a person's hand and go up to the blood stream to the speech center, where it creates "mind speech" in a natural voice. The FELICIA is not cumbersome nor takes much time for the person to use because the person speaks in real time. Unlike the late 20th and early 21st Centuries, where many doubt the validity of augmentative communication, especially FC, no one doubts FELICIA. When Keith sees and hears this, he wishes that Cleo could live in the 24th Century. He wishes that Cleo could communicate in real time with a FELICIA in his speech center. Cleo, who was nonverbal, used some sign and a PECS picture system.

For many sports in the 24th Century, especially killer hockey and triaggina, disabled and non-disabled play on the same team. Riaggina, which looks like a mixture between basketball and racquetball, can have teams that are unevenly matched, like a 2-man team against a 3-man team. Triaggina originated from the planet Carillon and became popular game on Earth, especially on college campuses.

Killer hockey is hockey played on sleds. It is rougher than regular hockey because players can rough-up each other without fear of being penalized. Even though the goal of killer hockey is to get the puck into the net, many come to see the players fight and rough each other up. Keith finds killer hockey too violent and prefers baseball because that sport is unchanged. Baseball is a game of history—so much so that in the 24th Century, Wrigley Field in Chicago has no lights.

At the beginning of his second year of living in the 24th Century, Keith meets his roommate and closest friend, Acirema Oscinarf. Before I go into how Keith met Acirema at the St. John of Kronstadt House of Industry (HOI) group home, let me digress into how Acirema came to live in Columbia, Missouri, from the city of Selegnasol, located on the planet Sckgoggi. Acirema is the youngest of five children of a solidly middle class Whole Number family. It was known only among the family and kept under wraps that a great-grandmother was a Fraction. The Oscinarf family knew that, if anyone found out, they would be considered Fractions, because if any Number had any Fraction ancestry, that Number is a Fraction. Also, when Acirema was born, his mother was aghast because he was born with a very pale, almost white skin and a weak cry, a sign of the chromosomal disorder, T-trisomy 24. All Numbers, Carillonian and Sckgoggian, have 50 chromosomes. If one is broken and the end of it is in the shape of a small "T," it is indicative of T-trisomy 24.

The effects of the disorder are light skin coloration (most Sckoggians are dark brown to blue black in coloration), small stature, and a range of developmental disabilities. Most have mental retardation (80%), and some can have autistic-like behaviors, Tourette's type of ticcing, echolalia and disjointed thought patterns. Acirema was one of the few with a normal IQ, but he had the short stature, light skin, and some tics, echolalia, and disjointed thought patterns. When Keith first met him, Acirema believed that American Indians were the descendants of the 12th tribe of Israel and that, if the 12th tribe was found, then he'd find Jesus. He even asked Keith if he was of the 12th tribe because Acirema always asked that question.

Before Acirema lived at the HOI group home, he lived in the US for ten years, working as an agricultural migrant worker in states like Texas, Arizona, and Florida with groups of Mexicans. (The big agribusiness corporations preferred to have their produce hand-picked because mechanized devices were considered not thorough enough.) These migrant workers were paid slave wages and lived in tents and had no rights. Acirema had no friends, learned Spanish, and was worked to exhaustion. Many times he, along with other workers, were deported to Mexico because occasionally the U.S. government would take a stand saying that agribusiness should not use slave labor or illegal aliens (Acirema was a legal alien because he was considered a refugee fleeing persecution). The deported workers would be deported to Mexico, sat in jails and were not allowed back in the U.S. Many of those who worked along the border were underpaid and overworked and assumed Acirema was Mexican because he spoke Spanish. The fact that Acirema was a Number was hardly noticed because there are Mexican Numbers and most likely the border workers didn't care. Also along the border were groups of nuns who took up the cause of the migrant workers' plight, and when they saw Acirema, they knew that he wasn't Mexican, that he had a disability, and that the Galactic Economic Union (GEU) had no influence on any Earth nations' policies concerning immigration and the movement of peoples.

Ever since Acirema came to the US, he believed that his sister Oneri was killed with the rest of his family, cut up and thrown into the Izeb River, when in fact she survived the massacre because early on, she played dead, thus saving herself from being chopped up. She had several injuries, and after they were healed, she came to the U.S. to live as an exile, fight for the rights of Fractions, and eventually go back to Selegnasol. Oneri moved to Columbia to be the head of the Peace and Justice Institute years after Acirema moved there. Since both of them believed each other to be dead, it surprised them to see each other unexpectedly in a lunch room on the Mizzou campus. Acirema was hysterical, so much so that the campus police (Campois) had to be called. Oneri didn't know what hit her, and Keith saw a flurry of action as the Campois dragged Acirema away, calling Oneri's name hysterically to the local jail. Eventually Acirema was let go on his recognizance with Keith's assurances that this wouldn't happen again and Oneri's testimony that, even though she had been assaulted, it was her long lost brother whom she thought was dead.

Keith has many other adventures in the 24th Century, both with Acirema and without him.

About the Author

My name is Kathy Grant. I have autism and live and work in Denver, Colorado. I am originally from St. Louis, Missouri, and come from a family of 8 (I am number 7). I lived at home until I was eighteen, and that was because I went to college and lived in a dorm for 4 years. I always went to regular schools and graduated from college in 1987 with a degree in Political Science. After college, I moved to New Jersey and was in an independent living program for 2.5 years and then moved back to Missouri.

In 1994, I married Raymond Grant. Unfortunately, the marriage ended in divorce in 1997, and I moved from St. Louis to Denver.

I have been involved in autism work since graduating college and was a Board Member for AUTCOM in the mid-90s. Now in 2003, I am a Board Member of the local autism chapter and have been asked to serve as a Board Member for AUTCOM starting in 2004. Kathy would be delighted to hear from you.

Reach her at woem_meoo_meow@yahoo.com

Anne creates a self portrait on her digital camera

Anne Carpenter

Thoughts on *The Speed of Dark*: Would I Want to be Cured of Autism?

Earlier this year, I read and reviewed a fascinating, yet chilling new science-fiction novel, *The Speed of Dark*, by Elizabeth Moon, who has a teenage son with autism. The protagonist, a 35-year old man named Lou Arrendale, has high-functioning autism and is living with it very successfully. He works at a pharmaceutical company analyzing computer algorithms for their various patterns, he drives a car, and his workplace has all the accommodations he could ever want and need: a gym, "spin-spirals" (motorized pinwheels of different colors), and his own private office, so that he knows where he is in space. Despite his naiveté in social situations, such as when his car is vandalized several times and he is almost killed, he has friends, and there is a young woman whom he likes. But he is faced with a terrible choice: an experimental new treatment that would completely alter his brain structure in such a way that he would no longer have "autism" but would be "cured" and would be a normal person. This prospect brought chills up and down my spine; it scared me. This sort of thing may become entirely possible with developments in genetic manipulation, nanotechnology (the use of micro-scopic computers) and psychopharmacology moving by leaps and bounds every day.

But this begs the question: What would happen if I were cured of autism? Would I be the same person? Would I *want* to be a different person?

Over the years, I have learned to adapt to having autism. I am realizing that, as it is a global movement and regulatory disturbance including thought, behavior, emotion, and sensory perception, one can find ways to accommodate the autism, including using visual schedules, checklists, breaking complex tasks down into smaller steps, and thinking about what one will say before saying it. This requires that one be aware of what he or she is doing *at all times* and constantly adjusting and readjusting the way things are done and how one handles various situations that come up. For example, if I get upset because the computer doesn't work correctly, due to Windows '98 or a virus, I just keep restarting the machine until it works or do something else, such as reading articles in a newsletter to see if they can be used for the newsletter, or reading one or two chapters of a new book. Then I try the computer again. This has worked for me, and if I wait long enough, the anger and panic subsides.

As people are exposed to different situations and challenges throughout their lives, they tend to change the way they behave in different situations. People with autism are no exception. As I have gotten older and more mature, I have gradually grown calmer and more adaptable. While I still have difficulty finding a solution to a problem right away and can still get panicky and anxious, I have been able to think about why that happened, to analyze the situation, then to find a solution to the problem at hand. I have been able to do this only because I have been included in different environments, such as regular classrooms, regular workplaces, and I haven't been in autistic classrooms, so I have been able to see how "the other half" lives. In addition, the supports I have had, including my mother's constant belief in me and her constant guidance and coaching in social skills, the job coaching that I have had from the director of the Autism Society of Michigan, the friendships and contacts I have had with different people at the Quaker Meeting that I attend, traveling to conferences and presenting, going to movies and other social events with family and friends, and attending events such as lectures at Borders bookstore, the Ann Arbor Art Fairs, and various lectures and social events held by the Quaker Meeting, have all helped me to develop social skills that I wouldn't have been able to master if I had been in a more sheltered environment.

Having autism, in which one's brain is wired differently, has allowed me to think in more creative ways. So when I get stuck on a problem and juggle ideas in my head, I can come up with a sudden flash of insight or a completely new idea. Having autism has other advantages as well. Because of the way my brain is wired, everything - sound, color, lights, smells - is heightened. When I was little, all of this was sheer torture. I felt like I was stuck in a kaleidoscope of never-ending colors, smells, and sounds that were too bright, too strong, too loud. Now, this heightened sensory awareness *enhances* my life. Everything seems interesting and wonderful to me—colors are brilliant and beautiful, lights are dazzling, music is melodious and tuneful, and fabrics such as silk, brushed cotton, and my fleece lavender jacket are wonderfully soft. This makes me enjoy life so much more, and the world is a richer, more wonderful place as a result.

If I were "cured" of autism, everything would be flatter and duller, and I wouldn't feel the joy and passion for certain things in quite the intense, wonderful way that I do now. Having autism allows me to be aware of and to appreciate minute details and subtle nuances that other people overlook, such as the rainbow inside a glass of white wine that I saw when it refracted the light in a restaurant and the beautiful patterns on a butterfly or beetle. This also allows me to find mistakes in the newsletter when I proofread it or to notice when something is wrong with a product so that I can return it and get a refund. Being "cured" or "normal" would deprive me of this ability. Having autism allows me to remember more things, such as telephone numbers or what places look like. If I see a phone number and write it down, I remember it for the rest of my life. Another advantage of having autism is persistence, which allows me to keep at a task or problem until it is completed or solved. This is considered an asset in the workplace and in school! In addition, my hair-trigger sensitivity to stimuli has allowed me to be very intuitive. I can usually "sense" when a situation may not work out or if the man I am dating is "Mr. Wrong." This has helped me to pick up on the more subtle social nuances that other people give off better than I was able to do when I was younger.

The most troubling question of all comes to mind: If I were "cured" of autism, I wouldn't be Anne Carpenter. Instead, I would be a whole different, unrecognizable person, with a whole different set of values, likes and dislikes, and sensory impressions, probably not as interesting and wonderful as what I have now. This is the big objection that many people with autism have to being "cured." They would not be themselves anymore. With the right accommodations and supports, the will and determination to grow and change, and tools and skills to work around the difficulties that autism can pose, one can do extraordinary things, such as design safer spacecraft to travel to distant galaxies, design vehicles that run on thought power alone, paint with paint that has millions of microscopic light emitting diodes that can be programmed to change colors, find a way to end war altogether, or devise an airplane that can get one from Detroit to Tokyo in three hours! The possibilities are endless, *without* a cure for autism.

About the Author

I was born in 1957 with Congenital Rubella Syndrome as a result of my mother's illness during her first trimester of pregnancy. At first, it was thought that I was spared the difficulties that it would present, but I was found to have cataracts, so my lenses were removed at two and three months of age, respectively. Then I had an open-heart valve repaired at seven months of age and had pink cheeks for the first time in my life! I was no longer a "blue baby." But other problems remained.

At first it was thought that my habit of flicking my fingers in front of my eyes and hand flapping were "blindisms," things that I did that were related to being blind. After being in a day program at the Children's Psychiatric Hospital in Ann Arbor (where I lived) to help me to learn to talk (I was still essentially nonverbal with a severe overall lag in development), I attended a class for blind and partially sighted children in a public school in a nearby community. I was mainstreamed part of the day in a regular classroom, and I stayed in that program until second grade, when I got a better prescription for eyeglasses because I was then able to tell the eye doctor what I could see on the eye chart. But because I couldn't communicate my feelings to my second grade teacher who I felt uncomfortable with, I behaved in challenging ways that upset her. As a result, she gave me a label of "emotionally disturbed," which landed me in a special education class of children with that label in my home community. After about a week-and-a-half, the teacher realized that I was in an inappropriate placement, so I was able to go to the regular classes and made a great deal of progress because I was included with typically developing students all the time. But I was very hyperactive, had great difficulty with sleep, physical coordination, and many sensory problems, so my mother looked into the possibility of sending me to a special school in Pennsylvania.

With a label of Minimal Brain Dysfunction (now ADHD), I attended the Pathway School from December, 1967, when

I was ten years old to August, 1970, when I was thirteen. Although I became calmer because of the setup of the school and the highly structured program, and I learned certain skills, my underlying condition of autism was not addressed, so I left while still having great difficulties with socialization, and, even though I was somewhat calmer, I would easily fly off the handle if the slightest thing went wrong. Despite that, I did well academically (except in math, which was very difficult for me), and I remained at Friends School in Detroit for four years, until I had finished my sophomore year of high school. After having attended a Quaker boarding school in Iowa where I only stayed one year and then attending a small alternative high school in Ann Arbor, I graduated from high school.

I went to what was then Grand Valley State College to their small alternative school, Thomas Jefferson College, where one could design one's own program with an advisor. I was more accepted by the students there because many of them had values that were different from those of the more traditional College of Arts and Sciences. I made a great deal of progress while in TJC and was admitted to library school. I graduated from Western Michigan University two years later, in 1982, but because I hadn't learned the skills I needed for the workplace, I was let go from a volunteer job at a local library.

I went to a community for adults with developmental disabilities in Virginia, which proved to be a very bad situation from the start. I lived with a couple who took their personal problems out on me. They didn't like the fact that I had a Master's degree in library science, yet behaved in a way that they didn't understand. In addition, I was placed in another sheltered workshop, where I continued to lose ground, so after a year-and-a-half of being in that community, I moved back to Ann Arbor, where I went to back to my Vocational Rehabilitation counselor. I got a job doing part-time newspaper indexing at home but was let go six months later because of problems with my supervisor and because I had not learned skills that I needed to keep a job.

After several other unsuccessful jobs, I was finally diagnosed with autism at the age of 30, in October of 1987, as a way to get Social Security benefits. Then doors started to open. I got my job with the Autism Society of Michigan (ASM) that spring. At first I did such duties as cataloging books and filing, but when the organization changed directors, I started presenting at ASM workshops, and I even presented at an Autism Society of America conference. Then our current director, Dr. Sally Burton-Hoyle, came aboard. We did Person-Centered Planning and decided that I would be best at writing articles and book reviews for the newsletter and doing Internet searches. These are the major part of my work at ASM, as well as telephone Information and Referral with parents, obtaining new books for the library, cataloging books, and presenting at conferences and workshops. Because the director presumes competence for <u>all</u> people with disabilities and because she has had high standards for me all along, I have continued to improve in my work. When I don't do as well as I should, she lets me know, and I resolve to do better, and I always do. At this point, I am continuing to find ways to work around autism, figuring out ways to compensate for any difficulties that it may present. There are setbacks, but after that come the successes. This has been done without the need for a cure for autism.

Anne can be contacted at acarpenter@provide.net

Chandima (Chammi) Rajapatirana

Waiting to Live

Every Day Lives Conference, 2002

We people with disabilities dream of leading everyday lives, lives in which we choose where we live and with whom, lives in which we choose how we work and how we play. But such lives are still dreams deferred for most of us. Waiting to make it happen is hard on anyone. It is especially hard on us disabled folks. We spend an awful amount of time waiting. Waiting for our abilities to be recognized, waiting for the supports we need. Waiting to live like everyday people.

Waiting for a voice is the hardest waiting of all. I did that for 18 years. Facilitated Communication, which enabled me to talk by typing, is what finally made it happen for me. Until then I was vested with the mantle of "profoundly retarded." Wearily, I tried to order my mouth to speak; my fingers to learn sign; my stubborn, brash body to move acceptably. However, autism is an awful prison and its fetters are unbreakable. Facilitated Communication loosened my fetters. Yet, I still struggle with autism hourly.

That we, Facilitated Communication users, must also struggle with skeptics compounds our misery. However, there are many of us now around the world. Isolated no more, we attend mainstream classes in schools and colleges. Some of us write books, most of us strive to type independently, and all of us yearn for everyday lives.

Working in the real world is an everyday thing to do. Aware that even the best writers had to earn a living while they waited for their writing to bring them fame and fortune, I started a lunch delivery business. I wanted something more than volunteer work and repetitive tasks. It took a lot of creative thinking and support from my team to do this. My mom provides the kind of enlightened support that makes this creativity possible. Is it possible to make an everyday life happen without enlightened support, the kind of support that will try determinedly to hear and honor our requests?

We, like you, want to pursue life, liberty, and happiness. Is it life if liberty and happiness are absent? Yet, that is what many of us have to settle for, life without liberty or happiness, which is not life at all. We need support from non-disabled people to make our dreams come true. We need laws to protect us and our rights. We need technology to find the accommodations we seek, researchers to look for the answers to the questions we ask. Above all, we need a community that makes all this happen.

It heartens me to see all of you today. I know we are in this together. I assure you that I appreciate all that has been achieved. Still we have a long trek ahead. Waiting to live is no way to live.

Further Reading

Many books have been written by people who experience life on the autism spectrum, and more are being written. The Autism National Committee Bookstore (AutCom Bookstore) makes a point of including these books. To access the AutCom Bookstore, go to the website of the Autism National Committee (www.autcom.org) and click on Bookstore, which will take you to the bookstore of the University of New Hampshire's Institute on Disability. (You may also go directly to this site: iodserver. unh.edu/iodbookstore/) In addition to their own bookstore, they manage the AutCom Bookstore.

Once at this site, look at the left-hand column called Shop by Category. AutCom Bookstore is second on this list. Click on it to browse and shop at the AutCom Bookstore.